THE MANY LIVES OF MISS K.

THE MANY LIVES OF
⬥ MISS K. ⬥

Toto Koopman—Model, Muse, Spy

Jean-Noël Liaut

Translated from the French by Denise Raab Jacobs

First published in the United States of America in 2013
By Rizzoli Ex Libris, an imprint of
Rizzoli International Publications, Inc.
300 Park Avenue South
New York, NY 10010
www.rizzoliusa.com

Originally published in France as *La Javanaise*
© Editions Robert Laffont, S.A., Paris, 2011
© 2013 Rizzoli International Publications, Inc.

2013 2014 2015 2016 / 10 9 8 7 6 5 4 3 2 1

Distributed in the U.S. trade by Random House, New York
Printed in U.S.A.

ISBN-13: 978-0-8478-4129-5
Library of Congress Catalog Control Number: 2013934993

For Floc'h, with affection

"I am more jealous of my own secrecy than of anything in this world. I hate discussing topics that might furnish people with clues about me. I do not want people to get to know me; rather that this should happen, I will build an extra fortress of reserve round myself, I will treble the guard at the gate "

Violet Trefusis
Letter to Vita Sackville-West,
August 27, 1918

"What does not warrant a second reading does not exert lasting fascination."

Cristina Campo

Introduction

"It's *Mademoiselle*! I never wanted to marry," countered Catharina "Toto" Koopman to anyone who dared to address her as *Madame*. It was the same answer she gave throughout her life, a long life of adventure, peril, conflict and intrigue; a life where petty rancor and timid imagination had no place and simplistic dualism had no voice—the extraordinary journey of a beguiling woman.

A stunning combination of the British fictional heroines Modesty Blaise and the Madonna of the Sleeping Cars, Toto Koopman (1908–1991) was the first biracial fashion model to achieve celebrity; she was also a spy, deported for her participation in the Résistance, and the muse for Europe's most influential art gallery of the second half of the 20th century. From the island of Java to the studios of *Vogue*, from the Ravensbrück concentration camp to the London art scene of the 1950s and 1960s, this beautiful, multilingual, daring, playful and resolutely free-spirited woman left no one indifferent.

While some thought her dissolute and arrogant, others considered her loyal and irresistible. Toto Koopman routinely defied convention in her search for love and adventure. Indifferent to social taboos, she had lovers of both sexes—from Tallulah Bankhead to Lord Beaverbrook—before settling down with Erica Brausen, the visionary German woman who launched the career of artist Francis Bacon. The two women remained together for the rest of their lives. From 1947 to 1973, their art gallery represented the most important contemporary painters and sculptors and played a vital role in the history of art and aesthetics.

While parts of Toto Koopman's life may seem to strain credibility, they are all true. Indeed, I believe many more facts concerning our beautiful and eccentric heroine have yet to be revealed. Capturing her essence for this biography was like trying to extinguish the burning bush—she remained elusive in every sense of the term.

Toto Koopman's life story had the "Lubitsch touch," meaning that the cast of sophisticated hucksters, double agents, fickle lovers, éminences grises and luminaries around her could have stepped out of one of that director's films. Reality can sometimes surpass fiction: a bogus Russian princess who married the son of Arthur Conan Doyle, a war hero who became the patron of the Royal Opera House in Covent Garden and a woman who was a sworn enemy of Chairman Mao were among the people who influenced her destiny. Both Toto Koopman and Erica Brausen followed the teachings of the esoteric philosopher G.I. Gurdjieff and, for more than ten years, maintained a profound and volatile relationship with Francis Bacon. All those drawn into Toto's circle lived by André Breton's belief that "even the slightest loss of impetus could prove fatal."

As I learned more about Toto Koopman, I was reminded of the "marching forest" in *Macbeth*. As the theme of a previous book I had written, the *angel of the bizarre* had been my longtime companion, and I was intrigued. Little did I know that my journey would take me across Europe, that I would consult the archives of the Chanel Conservatory as well as those from the Paris Prefecture of Police, that I would correspond with the Dutch intelligence service and that the people I interviewed would include the prize-winning writer Edmonde Charles-Roux, renowned gallerist Denise René and the pioneering director Peter Brook, among others.

Toto Koopman's life was an adventure, played with style and audacity. She was a phoenix whose multiple transformations evoke the heroines in Ovid's *Metamorphoses*. Following her trail led me from the ateliers of Max Beckmann and Joseph Oppenheimer, for whom she posed, to the 1936 Berlin Olympic Games, resurrecting such international spies as Moura Budberg and Stewart Menzies, the "M" made famous by the James Bond adventures; and when Toto's interest turned to archaeology and she participated in several digs, her mentor was none other than Max Mallowan, husband of Agatha Christie.

I traveled back in time to the set of an Alexander Korda film featuring Toto, Douglas Fairbanks and Merle Oberon. I discovered Panarea, one of the Aeolian Islands in the Tyrrhenian Sea. By transporting soil and water by boat from Naples, Toto transformed the volcanic and arid island into a veritable Eden, where she then held open-air salons with Luchino Visconti and Bruce Chatwin. Her multiple arrests during the period from 1941 to 1945 led to even more astounding revelations. Had the *femme fatale* become a knight-errant?

And what to make of the rumors that circulated about her? It was said that Miss K. was the only woman ever admitted as a member to White's, London's most exclusive gentlemen's club; that she owed her release from the Ravensbrück concentration camp to Raoul Wallenberg, one of the Righteous Among the Nations; and that, at age seventy, she was pressured by the Mafia to leave the island of Panarea.

Her life, marked by an unrelenting quest for independence, and replete with romance, humor and heartbreak, deserved to be known. More than standing as a portrait of an individual woman, this book traces the history of twentieth-century Europe: colonialism—the biracial child was one of Java's "green Dutchmen"—fascism, concentration camps, café society, artistic and aesthetic revolutions . . . In Toto Koopman, the intimate melds with the currents of history.

1

Toto Koopman remained discreet about certain events in her past, but she was eager to share childhood memories with her closest friends. Born in the shadows of the Buddhist temple of Borobudur, on the island of Java in Indonesia, Toto maintained that the sight of the temple's cupola was one of her earliest recollections. A slight exaggeration, perhaps, but Toto was always drawn to things bright and unusual rather than what Dante referred to as "the lukewarm." She had mastered the process of selective memory by erasing whatever was bland and ordinary, filtering her own reality and remaining indifferent to everyday triviality.

Toto's friends remember her descriptions of grand colonial homes, lush gardens and servants wearing exotic uniforms; stories about her great-grandmother, of Javanese and Chinese ancestry, who had perhaps been part of the Sultan of Solo's harem. But the dominant figure in her personal Pantheon was her father, an officer in the Dutch cavalry, a man so fond of his horses that the only name that came to his mind when his daughter was born was that of his favorite mount, Toto. The registry rejected his choice and the child was officially given the name Catharina—though she would always be known as Toto.

Because of her father's military career, Toto's family moved frequently. One of her favorite homes was in the small mountain garrison town of Salatiga, in the heart of Java, where the officers' residences were built around a vast lawn and surrounded by trees. In the lawn's center stood a gazebo where, twice each week, an orchestra played military music. These performances concluded with torch-lit parades.

Despite a lifelong nostalgia for the landscape of tea plantations and rice fields, Toto never failed to mention that the area she grew up in was so remote that there was neither electricity nor telephone service. To reach the nearest train station, the Koopman family had to travel for several hours in a stagecoach that was similar to those used in the American West.

With the outbreak of World War I, news from Europe grew scarce and Salatiga felt even more isolated. Toto's brother had been sent to boarding school in Holland right before the war, and her parents could not conceal their anxiety. Even at a young age, Toto understood her parents' anguish at the thought of their son, on his own and so close to the chaos unfolding around him. She also understood that their feelings of guilt caused them to indulge her every whim.

Home schooled, Toto spent her free time playing with her many pets. She looked after cats, dogs, rabbits, dwarf chickens and even a kangaroo that her father had brought home from Australia. "Toto told me that she had a baby elephant, an incredibly exotic notion when compared to our dull English childhoods," remembered Lady Deirdre Curteis. The elephant was a gift to Colonel Koopman from the King of Siam, following the king's visit to Java when the colonel had served as his aide-de-camp. Toto was only able to keep the elephant for a short time; he drank so much milk the family could not meet his needs, and eventually he was taken to the closest zoo. Shortly before her death, Miss K. confided that she had experienced sorrow for the first time upon losing her pet elephant.

Every morning, Toto and her mother rose early and rode their bicycles to a nearby lake. Surrounded by high rocks, the small lake was fed by a stream that had its source on the highest peaks of the island and cascaded down in a fierce waterfall before reaching the ground. Toto learned to swim in these waters, supported at first by a stalk of bamboo tucked under each arm to keep her afloat. Eventually, she relied on only one stalk, and when she felt ready, the little girl went in on her own, rapidly becoming an excellent swimmer.

To reach the lake, Toto and her mother would leave their bicycles near the gate of a large house and follow a narrow path down to the water. On the way back, along this same path, they often encountered an old Chinese man. This particularly well-mannered man was the owner of an unusual home that resembled an immense pagoda redesigned by a Victorian architect. The three would exchange a few words, and the man often gave the young girl sweets or small gifts. Toto could not have imagined that years later, in Paris, she would become very close to the daughter of this discreet and reserved man who headed an immense commercial empire with branches throughout China and other parts of the Far East.

Most shops in Salatiga were owned by the Chinese, except for one, Toto's favorite: that shop belonged to a Japanese concern and was filled with bright-colored toys and inexpensive baubles. Colonel Koopman was convinced that the owner was not really a shopkeeper but a Japanese officer who was spying on the activities of the Dutch army. Toto never forgot that rumor and her friends believed it played a key role in her imagination.

On Saturday afternoons, the young Toto often went to the movies. She adored serial adventures with recurring heroes, especially *The Perils of Pauline*, starring Pearl White. While the film was being projected, an accompanist played an old mechanical piano, his feet pressing the pedals furiously at each new dramatic development. The Chinese and Javanese audience, along with the children seated in the balcony, cheered each time Pearl White pulled off one of her famous escapes. Several years later, Toto was thrilled to meet the actress, who was living in a château on the outskirts of Paris; the admiration she had felt as a child was validated when she learned that White was an accomplished horsewoman who had performed most of her own stunts.

Horseback riding was a regular activity for the Koopman family. They rode robust Australian horses whose names—Veteran, Fighter, Soldier and Victory—revealed a great deal about the colonel's mindset during this time of war. Toto's mother rode sidesaddle and wore a white linen riding habit, a detail that Miss K., always sensitive to the power of an image, would never forget.

Toto dreaded riding; she was terrified and fell often. After she broke her hip in a serious fall, she was no longer required to ride. Colonel Koopman's dream of his daughter becoming a great horsewoman was never realized. Occasionally, Australian jockeys came to ride the horses, and those jockeys taught Toto her first English words.

Growing up, Toto became very attached to the family's Javanese servants. Years later, during the Japanese occupation, many household servants hid their former employers and the children they had raised like their own. Toto often said that her *baboe* Djim—*baboe* is the Indonesian word for nanny—would have done the same for her. Miss K. felt enormous affection for this tiny and protective woman, and decades later she still recalled the most precise details about Djim: her perfectly starched and colorful *kabajas*, or jackets; her teeth, planed with a file and nearly jet black from chewing betel nut; and her earlobes, pierced with holes the size of small coins to accommodate enormous earrings. The male servants wore intricately tied batik turbans, and the little girl liked to watch how they folded the fabric into perfect knots.

Toto described her parents' sartorial elegance in great detail. Despite the heat and humidity, the colonel and Mrs. Koopman were always impeccably dressed and groomed. At home, Toto's mother wore traditional Javanese clothing, all in white, like her linen riding costumes. After their morning swims, Mrs. Koopman returned home to change. She secured her lace-trimmed chiffon *kabaja* with three jeweled pins held together with thin gold or silver chains that always made Toto think of alpine climbers tied to each other for safety. When her father was not in uniform, he wore an immaculate white cotton suit, with the jacket buttoned to the neck; years later the uniforms worn by Swiss train conductors would remind Toto of this outfit. Toto always liked to add an exotic element to her descriptions, such as the fact that all their furniture was made of very hard wood because of the colonies of white ants that devoured everything in their path.

The Javanese were highly superstitious and well versed in magic and occult practices. Toto spoke at length about their customs and never failed to recount one particular incident that took place when she was visiting a friend of her mother's who owned a coffee plantation and collected very rare Japanese weapons. The friend's most prized piece was a javelin that rested on a red lacquer stand; the servants considered it a sacred object and never failed to bow when passing before it.

The hostess, concerned for Toto's safety around these objects, decided to put her collection away in a dark storage room. During the first night of her stay, Toto was awakened by the sounds of a crying infant, yet there were no newborns in the household. The same phenomenon occurred every night thereafter, and when Toto reported that the sobs were coming from the small storage room, the servants panicked. They were convinced that the sacred javelin was expressing its sorrow and loneliness, and that if it remained in seclusion, disaster inevitably would strike the household. The javelin was then returned to its place in the main reception room, where it regained its *joie de vivre,* and the crying ceased. Toto's *baboe,* Djim, assured Toto that the javelin would watch over her forever, and later Toto believed she had survived the death camps because of its protection.

2

Toto was a gifted storyteller, and when listening to her tales her friends often felt transported to the world of *The River*, Rumer Godden's story of a young English woman's adventures in Bengal, and the inspiration for one of Jean Renoir's finest films. Miss K. could deftly set a scene, but her recollections were not always an accurate depiction of her life in Java. She often adjusted the facts to suit her fancy.

Stories about white ants devouring the furniture and the occult practices of the Javanese are far more intriguing than facts such as dates, places and occupations. One hopes the spirit of Miss K. will forgive us for dwelling for a moment on those prosaic details.

Catharina Johanna Anna Koopman was born on October 28, 1908 in Salatiga, on the island of Java in Indonesia. Situated in the foothills below the Merbabu and Telomoyo volcanoes, between Semarang, the capital of the province of Central Java, and the royal city of Yogyakarta, Salatiga was actually not near the Borobudur temple, as Toto claimed. Associating her birthplace with this majestic temple, built in the 8th and 9th centuries to honor the teachings of Buddha, was typical of our heroine, who considered making an impression all-important.

Her father, Jan George Koopman, was born in Indonesia in 1878 and was a colonel in the cavalry regiment of the Dutch East Indies army. He was in charge of acquiring horses in Australia for the troops stationed in Java. Colonel Koopman married Catharina Johanna Westrik, who was born in 1880, also in Indonesia. Unlike her husband, who was of pure Dutch descent, Catharina was half-Indonesian and had Chinese ancestors—an extremely significant fact. The Dutch had colonized Indonesia at the end of the 16th century, and there was intense prejudice toward the biracial population. Mrs. Koopman and her children were considered "green Dutchmen," a derogatory reference to the color of their skin.

Still, Toto painted an idyllic picture of that time, never mentioning the issue of segregation or racial prejudice. Were her parents truly able to shield Toto and her brother, Henri, from the blatant racism? The family was indeed very close, and Colonel and Mrs. Koopman must have done their best to protect their family from the hostility that settlers directed toward all biracial citizens—hostility that by all accounts was extremely virulent.

Toto was very proud of her ethnicity, speaking openly of it at a time when such an attitude was rare. In London in the early 1930s, Merle Oberon, fearful that the press would reveal that her mother was Indian, tried to pass the woman off as her maid. At the same time in the very same city, Toto, who was filming a movie with Oberon, made a point of telling the press that she was half-Javanese, when in truth she was only one quarter-Indonesian.

Toto's friend Hui-Lan Wellington-Koo was also born and raised in Java. In her memoir, *No Feast Lasts Forever*, published in 1975, she wrote that racism was only one of many problems on the island. She was contemptuous of the Dutch settlers and their widespread corruption, merciless exploitation of a cheap and uneducated labor force and complete refusal to improve the economy of the region if it did not profit them directly. In indignant prose, she provided a long list of grievances against the settlers. Hui-Lan, of Chinese descent, was one of the twenty-six recognized children of sugar magnate Oei Tiong Ham. While Miss K. had fond memories of Hui-Lan's father, who had been her neighbor by the lake, the two women did not meet until 1936, when they became close friends in Paris.

A comparison of their respective memories reveals a great deal about Toto Koopman's priorities. One's hell was the other's paradise. "Toto, who suffered the worst fate on this earth in the concentration camps, never complained about anything. She cast a resolutely sunny look on the past," recalled Lady Deirdre Curteis. "Each experience, traumatic as it might have been, served as a lesson for her own evolution, and she chose to remember only the good. Still, she had no illusions and nobody was less naïve. I do believe that the years she spent in Java were indeed very happy ones."

The images in family photo albums confirm Toto's recollections: her mother riding sidesaddle, her father in uniform, the servants, the lush gardens and Toto herself—always smiling—wearing a caftan or jodhpurs, holding a riding crop, accompanied by her white Afghan hound. "She adored her brother," remembered F.C., a British friend. "I always believed, from what she said, that there was a special bond between them." Henri Lodewijk George Koopman was also born in Salatiga, in 1902, and the two children were inseparable. According to Henri Koopman's son, Robbert J.B. Koopman, "Toto and Ody, our nickname for our father, loved each other deeply and always respected each other's lifestyle choices."

But the most revealing clues lay elsewhere. Many of Miss K.'s memories of her years in Java explain the person she became as an adult. Pearl White had become a wildly popular actress after starring in the twenty episodes of *The Perils of Pauline*. In each episode, a young, independent and courageous woman faced extraordinary challenges and extricated herself from the most perilous situations without ever losing any of her charm and elegance.

Watching these films, Toto, who was just a little girl at the time, developed an adventurous and cinematic perspective on her own existence. "She truly lived the life of a *film noir* vamp," recalled F.C. "A cover girl turned secret agent who joined the Résistance, survived the hell of a concentration camp and then became an archaeologist! Her story could rival those of all the heroines played by Pearl White, her childhood idol. And those Japanese spies! She relished the atmosphere of intrigue and mystery, as evidenced by her own life story."

Similarly, Toto was profoundly influenced by the occult beliefs that were such a deeply rooted part of the island's culture. She reveled in concepts that defied all rational explanation, and the hermetic and secret connections between spirits and humans. Her interest in the subject continued throughout her life. As an adult, she consulted astrologists, and after World War II she embraced the spiritual philosophy of G.I. Gurdjieff.

In 1920, at the age of twelve, Toto left Java to attend Bloemendaal boarding school in Holland, an institution known for its academic excellence. Later, she recalled that when Princess Juliana, who would become queen of the Netherlands in 1948, came to the school to present awards and diplomas, the children wore ceremonial uniforms.

Her favorite subjects were literature, history and geography, and she had an extraordinary gift for learning foreign languages. By the age of sixteen, she was fluent in Dutch, French, English and German. She then mastered Italian and, to a lesser degree, Turkish. (After boarding school, Toto went on to complete her studies at a finishing school in England, the traditional path at the time for a girl from a good family.)

While Toto was far from home and from her parents, who remained in Java, she was not lonely; she spent every weekend with a dear friend of her mother's who happened to live near the boarding school. Toto became very close to the woman's two eldest daughters, who traveled extensively and regularly visited Paris. They brought back the latest Parisian fashions and trends—*gamine* haircuts and flesh colored stockings—which Toto adopted immediately. This always caused a stir among her fellow students, who still sported heavy braids and dark leggings. Even then, Toto's behavior was considered improper. But Miss K. was undaunted and thought only of the day when she would be able to move to Paris, far from the Dutch atmosphere of austerity.

3

Had Toto Koopman been ugly, her life would have turned out quite differently. The word "beauty" comes up at the mere mention of her name, whether in conversation or in print. Such was the fascination she elicited from all those who met her that even when discussing the most difficult period of her life, people feel compelled to mention her alluring appearance. Professor Raoul Tubiana, a renowned French hand surgeon and the last person one could accuse of superficiality, was one of many who fell under her spell. He described her as "Ava Gardner's double, deported to Ravensbrück for espionage."[1]

When Toto first arrived in Paris in 1928, she knew she had the looks to conquer the world's capital of elegance. Though she was a foreigner and had no money or connections, her youth, beauty and independent spirit made her feel invincible. At nineteen, she had completed her studies and moved away from her family, and she was eager to find a job and become financially independent. Toto started modeling almost immediately. Before signing on exclusively for *Vogue*, she worked for some less prestigious mail-order catalogues that sold patterns and fabric.

Toto's parents were understandably displeased with her career choice: modeling was a socially unacceptable occupation, with connotations of immorality. A model fell somewhere between a cabaret dancer and a tart. A young woman of Toto's standing was expected to marry, raise children and stay at home. But Toto was as unconcerned with convention as she was with the opinions of others. She believed life offered infinite possibilities, and she intended to take full advantage of her freedom without having to account to anyone—quite an audacious attitude for 1928, when British women had just obtained the right to vote and Amelia Earhart had recently crossed the Atlantic by plane. Such victories were still scarce.

With her modest earnings, Toto rented a small apartment at 108 boulevard Berthier, in the 17th arrondissement, the sort of Parisian neighborhood often described in atmospheric detail by the writer Léon-Paul Fargue. It was not a prestigious address, but interesting people, including Yvette Guilbert, the cabaret singer immortalized by Henri de Toulouse-Lautrec, and Arletty, the future film star, also lived on boulevard Berthier. In any case, Toto was out day and night and just needed a place to sleep. As soon as she could afford to, she began to live in hotels, which suited her nomadic spirit.

An astonishing number of *grands couturiers*—more than eighty—were at work in Paris at the time. The most famous among them were Madeleine Vionnet, Jeanne Lanvin and Gabrielle "Coco" Chanel. On June 23, 1930, Toto was hired as a house model for Chanel, marking her entry into that exclusive world of luxury and refinement. With her dark hair, slightly slanted green eyes and perfect proportions, the tall and slender Toto had all the features that appealed to Mademoiselle Chanel.

Chanel, "the exterminating angel of 19th-century French style," as her friend Paul Morand described her, had conceived a new way of dressing, offering her clients a freedom of movement they had never known before. By reinterpreting the uniform she had worn as an orphan, Chanel created the most famous garment in the history of fashion, the little black dress. With her distaste for restrictions as guiding force, the *couturière* created a completely modern wardrobe that borrowed pants from sailors, jerseys from jockeys and austere capes from American YMCA volunteers. Toto personified the Chanel ideal—a woman about town, one who had a job and defined her own fashion. Miss K. was the perfect incarnation of the contemporary woman during the period between the two wars.

Chanel was admired, imitated and feared for her biting remarks: "I am the only Auvergne volcano that is not extinct," she is said to have claimed in 1930. Colette accurately captured the designer's combative spirit: "In her butting energy, in her way of facing up to things, of listening, in the defensiveness that sometimes raises a barricade across her face, Chanel is a black bull."[2] As queen bee, Coco demanded absolute compliance from her three thousand workers—something that proved impossible for Miss K.

Toto remained at Chanel for only six months; she left the rue Cambon store on November 6, 1930. During that time, she appeared in only one fashion show, the one for the 1930–1931 fall/winter collection, which featured sober antelope coats and fluid evening dresses with backs that evoked peacock tails. What had transpired between the two women that caused such a hasty departure? When pressed on the subject, Toto answered that she did not like the way Chanel touched her during the fittings. Had Mademoiselle Chanel made unwelcome advances? No one knew for sure; Toto was expert at keeping her answers vague.

Rather than give in to Chanel's domineering attitude, Toto, who abhorred any form of authority, chose to leave. Colette captured the kind of sensual violence Coco could display when she described how a model "totters occasionally under the two creative, severe, kneading arms that press against it. . . . Sometimes

[Chanel] falls to her knees before her work and grasps it, not to worship but to punish it again."[3] This environment proved intolerable for Toto, who relished her independence. She rarely dwelled on the time she had spent at the rue Cambon store and returned only in the 1960s to buy one of the designer's famous tweed suits.

Toto found another job right away. She went to work for Marcel Rochas, who was known for his masculine-inspired pants and beach pajamas. She also worked with the French-American designer Mainbocher, who had opened his *maison de couture* on avenue Georges-V in 1930. Each fashion house had a distinctive style that extended to the décor of its salons—a blue and white color scheme for Rochas, and numerous gold-framed mirrors, zebra skins and Nymphenburg porcelain for Mainbocher. Toto was always attracted to remarkable people, and Mainbocher became her favorite designer. He was a World War I hero who had dismantled a network of drug traffickers that had been supplying narcotics to American aviators, all the while pretending to be a mild-mannered music student—a very credible cover, as he had a beautiful baritone voice.

Toto preferred working for men—whether they were heterosexual like Marcel Rochas or homosexual like Mainbocher. She was involved in all aspects of the collections and brought the designs to life. She modeled for the press shows but also each afternoon for the houses' clients. In addition, she posed for illustrators and photographers in outfits that were created especially for her.

The designers recognized her charisma and gladly lent Miss K. day and evening dresses. She became their "jockey," the term used for a young woman—model, actress or socialite—who wore their "colors," representing them in Parisian society. And Toto was everywhere: at the opera, at the Longchamp and Auteuil racecourses for the *pesages*, in nightclubs such as Chez Bricktop and at galas hosted by Jean Patou. During the summer of 1930, for the occasion of his Silver Ball, Patou had all the trees in his garden covered with thousands of aluminum leaves.

Driven by an irrepressible exuberance and uninhibited desire for the unusual, Toto was always seeking the next thrill. Famous in her milieu was Barbette at the Medrano Circus: the public was stunned when the platinum-haired acrobat, a female impersonator, removed his wig at the end of each performance. All of Paris society, with Jean Cocteau at its helm, swooned at such originality and applauded wildly.

"It was like another world," Toto confided in 1976 to the journalist Brigid Keenan. "People always dressed in the evenings. If you were working like me you would rush home, bathe and then dress yourself up—and I really *mean* dress up.... There was always an in place to be seen at. We were all exhibitionists, show-offs." Toto, who had an extremely theatrical vision of herself, casually revealed the secret of her elegance: "One dressed up not to please men, but to astound the other women."[4]

Toto was always attracted to wild and fanciful characters. Her nightlife became more frenzied than ever when she became involved with the astonishing Mdivani family.

4

"I am the only father to have inherited a title from his children!" laughed General Zakhari Mdivani, speaking of his boisterous offspring. Mostly forgotten today, the Mdivani clan was the talk of Paris in the 1920s and 1930s. Their cleverly staged antics generated a great deal of press and caught the attention of even the most indifferent onlookers. Countless fantastic stories unfolded as a result of the Russian Revolution but none rivaled the frenzy and theatrics of the Mdivani saga.

The Mdivani brothers, Alexis, David and Serge, and their sisters, Nina and Roussy, took Paris by storm. Their good looks and noble status—dubious as it was—instantly captivated the Parisian society they fully intended to exploit. "They were very dramatic and very funny at the same time," recalled Denise Tual, a close friend of Roussy. "At first, before the brothers married film stars and heiresses, they played the chic pauper game. In the middle of a soirée, these wildly handsome men in tuxedos would suddenly take their leave, claiming they had to report to the garage where they earned their livelihood. A click of the heels and they were gone. Their sisters wore luxurious gypsy-style gowns and were equally irresistible, especially Roussy, who was stunning. She professed to be uneducated, that she could neither read nor write and had to sign documents with an X. Parisian snobs were smitten by their larger than life personalities and by the stories they recounted about their past that simply defied imagination."

While the Mdivani brothers were not commoners —their father had served as the last tsar's aide-de-camp—they were not princes either, though they mentioned the title repeatedly and deftly parlayed it to their advantage. Their exile had initially put them in difficult financial circumstances, but it is questionable whether Alexis and Roussy really were reduced to shining shoes in the streets of Istanbul as they claimed. One also wonders whether they lived on their own as ragamuffins among the sailors and orphans of the Bosphorus. Soon after arriving in France, the brothers became famous for their sexual prowess. While still an adolescent, Alexis became lovers with the *chanteuse* Mistinguett, and she was an expert in this area.

By the early 1930s, the family had managed to amass a vast fortune thanks to advantageous unions.

Nina, the smartest of the siblings, was Toto's closest friend, and Alexis, the most handsome brother, was Toto's lover. Rebaptized "the marrying Mdivanis," Serge and David wed Hollywood stars Pola Negri and Mae Murray; Alexis sold his title to Louise Astor Van Alen, one of the wealthiest heiresses in the United States, who was thrilled to become a princess.

Roussy, meanwhile, made her own headlines when she formed an unlikely *ménage à trois* with the Catalan painter José Maria Sert and his wife, Misia. The trio was the inspiration for Jean Cocteau's *Les Monstres Sacrés*. Sert, also know as the "Tiepolo of the Ritz" and affluent in his own right, eventually left his wife to marry the younger Mdivani sister. Nina carefully orchestrated these unions with the help of her first husband, an American attorney, whom she later divorced to marry the son of Sir Arthur Conan Doyle; she had hoped to profit from the spectacular royalties generated by the worldwide success of the Sherlock Holmes series. Toto, who disliked anything unremarkable, considered the Mdivanis to be demigods among common men. She longed to be one of them. The affection was mutual, and the clan soon folded her into its ranks.

How many men and women shared Toto's favors? Nobody can say, and it matters little. She was open about her bisexuality and physical love was as natural to her as breathing. Luckily, Miss K. acknowledged, she never became pregnant or contracted a venereal disease. What is certain is that she cared deeply for Alexis and that her unmarried lifestyle was considered very risqué for a woman in those times.

Alexis, three years her senior, was not a stable companion. Theirs was an open relationship, the "exchange of two fantasies and the contact of two bodies," to use an epigram by the French writer Nicolas Chamfort. Toto, for whom dullness and boredom were anathema, was enchanted by the princely bad boy whose intensity matched her own. Alexis had the devil in him and was incapable of moderation. When he was not playing polo with the Prince of Wales and Lord Mountbatten, he was hosting elaborate balls in his *hôtel particulier* on the place des États-Unis. Those *fêtes* were funded by his charming and rarely seen wife—the wife Alexis soon divorced in order to marry, in 1933, Barbara Hutton, the most sought-after heiress in the United States. Nothing, not even cosmic disturbances could disrupt his glittering world of excitement. While the rest of the planet was reeling from the economic crash of 1929, Alexis basked in complete insouciance.

Alexis was flamboyant in every aspect of his life, including the intense, some would say quasi-incestuous, relationship he maintained with his sister Roussy. One particularly colorful story had them circling the place de la Concorde, holding hands while riding side by side in their respective sports cars. Repelled by any kind of physical or sentimental mawkishness, Toto instead favored style and ironic detachment. The Mdivani brothers were tuxedo-clad hooligans, devious pleasure-seeking predators. In their company, she redefined her own sense of freedom.

Revelling in the presence of both her angels and her demons, enjoying money without the tethers of guilt, giving *to* but never *of* herself, keeping gloom at a safe distance. While this lifestyle struck many as chaotic and excessive, Miss K. considered it an expression of intellectual and erotic independence.

Her friendship with the Mdivanis was also an apprenticeship in the rules of European society of the early 1930s. She quickly learned the arcane ways of the social ecosystem and how to play the game. At that time, a title, even a dubious one, was a valuable commodity, and Toto didn't hesitate to follow the Mdivani example by inventing her own: she became the Baroness van Halmaëll, and even registered her passport under that name. "After an extensive search to uncover any noble lineage in our family," revealed her nephew Robbert J.B. Koopman, "she finally came upon Jan George Koopman (1770–1830), who had married Maria van Halmaëll (1772–1825). The van Halmaëlls were a wealthy Belgian family of minor nobility from the Liège area who had been granted knighthood."

It is easy to understand why Alexis Mdivani and his siblings were drawn to Toto. She was beautiful, free-spirited, open-minded and self-assured. Like them, she was tireless and lived at full speed. Never one to accept frustration, Miss K. wrote her own rules, and without ever relinquishing her femininity she adopted a social and sexual autonomy previously reserved only for men. She was both sister-in-arms and siren to Alexis. Their relationship was based solely on shared sensuality and imagination; it was free of blackmail and ultimatums. They could have adopted as their own the motto of the Prince of Ligne: "Together if we choose—apart if we're bored."

In Paris, Toto and Alexis were out every night. In the summer, they went to Spain to visit the Serts. They sailed on board the *Ali-Baba*—the luxurious yacht that had been a gift from Alexis's father-in-law, Franklyn Hutton: *Ali* stood for Alexis, *Baba* for Barbara. At the same time, Roussy was at the Mas Juny, the house that José had built for her on the Costa Brava, where she held court with a domesticated monkey perched on her shoulder. Surrounding oneself with such outlandish flamboyance can often mask a cruel reality: weakened by a life of idleness and cynicism, the narcissistic and unpredictable Alexis had become an alcoholic and suffered several nervous breakdowns. At the slightest frustration, he would throw himself on the ground and start shrieking.

Following his divorce in 1935 from Barbara Hutton, Alexis moved into a large apartment on the place du Palais-Bourbon. He chose an Indian décor: precious silk fabric on the walls, white satin banquettes and art objects imported at great cost from Rajasthan. His servants wore turbans—it was a home befitting his character. The apartment was within walking distance of Toto's new home, as she had given up her boulevard Berthier apartment for a hotel room on rue de l'Université. But the Mdivani saga would soon come to a tragic end.

In 1935, Alexis was decapitated in car accident. He was just thirty years old. A mere seven months later, Serge was killed during a polo match, his skull crushed by a horse after a fall. Roussy, who had shared such a special bond with Alexis, was shattered by grief and lost the will to live. Drugged, anorexic and ravaged by tuberculosis, she died in 1938, at the age of thirty-two. Toto would always remember Alexis with great fondness and remained close to Nina until she, too, died in 1987.

5

By 1932, Toto was working with George Hoyningen-Huene, one of the seminal photographers of his generation. A German friend of Toto's who was already working with Hoyningen-Huene introduced them, and Toto began posing for the photographer immediately. Today, those photographs of Toto are seen in museums, published in monographs and featured on postcards. Over the course of two years Hoyningen-Huene captured her true essence, and through his photographs she came to represent the aspirations of a new generation of women.

Hoyningen-Huene's father was a Baltic baron and head equerry in service to the tsar. Hoyningen-Huene fled Russia during the revolution and settled in Paris. Suddenly penniless, he tried his hand as a translator, a film extra and an illustrator for several magazines before turning to photography. He was an inspirational force at *Vogue* from 1926 to 1935. Toto, who always had a soft spot for Russians émigrés, had finally found her professional match.

Hoyningen-Huene's Russian background also influenced his artistic choices. As a young man, he had spent countless hours roaming the palaces and museums of St. Petersburg, absorbing the masterpieces they housed. He would always associate the elegance of the Imperial Court of Russia with the Greek and Roman statuary and Italian Renaissance painting he knew so well. Combining those references with the latest technical developments in photography and his acute sense of the times in which he lived, Hoyningen-Huene wanted to capture the spirit of the modern woman of the 1930s—but how? The question drove his work and to answer it he turned to his favorite models. Toto Koopman, along with Lee Miller and Lisa Fonssagrives, was part of that exclusive group.

"Ornament is crime," the battle cry of Austrian architect Adolf Loos, summed up the mood of 1932. Its impact was felt in many fields, from the buildings of Le Corbusier and Robert Mallet-Stevens to the spare interior designs of Jean-Michel Frank and Syrie Maugham to the creations of the top Parisian couturiers. Taking its cue from ancient Greece, the neoclassical form served as the foundation for the fashions of Madeleine Vionnet and her most famous disciple, Augustabernard.

The boyish or *garçonne* style, emblematic of the flapper era, was liberating but not particularly flattering. Vionnet believed a woman could retain that freedom of movement without giving up the elegance that had been lost along the way. By using the bias cut, she created fluid clothes that gently skimmed the body without any constraints. Vionnet met the needs of contemporary women with her own interpretation of antiquity: her modern-day Juno may have stepped straight out of the Parthenon, but this independent woman traveled by plane or automobile.

Still, one needed a manual to know how to wear her clothes. Often referred to as the "Euclid of fashion," Vionnet created garments with such elaborate construction that clients were often at a loss when it came to dressing themselves and frequently asked their private *vendeuses* to help them arrange the various panels and drapes at home before evenings out. Vionnet's deconstructed designs were often compared to cubist paintings.

Hoyningen-Huene considered Toto an ideal model for these ingeniously cut minimalist creations. The dresses hugged the curves of the body like a second skin, making it impossible to wear undergarments. To avoid indecency, Toto powdered her breasts and pubic area so that the fabric would not cling to those parts of her body.

A photo shoot was a true exchange between the photographer and his model. Every shot evoked a specific mood or state of mind. Hoyningen-Huene, in his own words, wanted to reveal the "inner beauty" of his subject, yet his photographs of Toto—suggesting a mood of quiet reflection and a hint of the enigmatic smile of a Khmer Buddha—were in sharp contrast to the turmoil of her private life.

Toto was the first biracial model to achieve celebrity. She was featured dozens of times in the different editions of *Vogue*, photographed by Hoyningen-Huene in black-and-white or in color when she appeared on the magazine's cover. Together, they created some of the most iconic photographs of that period, such as the one of Toto wearing an Augustabernard gown in the September 1933 issue of *Vogue*. In this shot, Toto is photographed from behind, years before Magritte would execute his *Portrait of Edward James* (1937), in which the subject is also seen from behind. Hiding one's face and revealing only the back of the neck and the curve of the hips was considered very provocative.

Toto also posed for Edward Steichen, Horst P. Horst and Cecil Beaton, but nobody caught her spirit the way Hoyningen-Huene did. In another photograph by the photographer, one that firmly established her reputation as a model in 1934, she is seen descending a staircase in what appears to be a Greek temple; once again, she is wearing a gossamer gown by Augustabernard. "A raking light from the left of the set accents Miss Koopman's pronounced cheekbones and creates a long, dark scimitar of shadow which sweeps back from the delicately poised hand," William E. Ewing wrote. "A shadow cast by the model's lithe body is framed by the pedestal; this shadow relates to the naked torso on the pedestal, thus titillating the viewer with a suggestion of Miss Koopman's thinly veiled nudity.... Nothing is left to chance in this remarkable image, in conception and execution one of Huene's most brilliant."[5] Indeed, it remains one of the most beautiful photographs in the history of fashion. "Great portrait photographers are great mythologists," observed Roland Barthes, who was mad about photography.

To meet his exacting demands, Hoyningen-Huene ran the *Vogue* studio on avenue des Champs-Élysées with an iron fist. He obsessed over every detail, staged every shot himself and chased away anyone who was not indispensable. The photographer demanded absolute silence on the set so that nothing would disrupt the hypnotic relationship he established with his models. It took hours to set up the perfect lighting, and Hoyningen-Huene considered using stand-ins to preserve his favorite models' strength. The heat on the stage was blistering, requiring his assistants to wear overalls, protective sunglasses and leather gloves in order to handle the lamps without getting burned.

The models had to pose for long periods of time, and he needed to hold their attention so as not to break the spell. In the aforementioned photograph, Toto appears to be caught by the camera just as she is quickly coming down the stairs, while in fact she had to remain still for a very long time, as the slightest movement would have ruined the shot. In his role as Pygmalion, Hoyningen-Huene photographed his Galatea from new angles, with unexpected effects and dramatic contrasts.

Outside of work, Miss K. spent little time with the other models, except for Lee Miller, with whom she remained close through the 1950s and 1960s. The young American was Man Ray's mistress in the 1930s and it was at his side that she learned the techniques of photography. Miller and Man Ray did not go unnoticed: it was rumored that they strolled through the streets of Paris attached to each other by a gold chain tied around their waists. Miller had obtained a dissected woman's breast from a medical school and carried it around with her on a plate. She featured it as the subject of a *nature morte*, adding a knife and fork and a set of salt and pepper shakers. Her surrealist sense of humor delighted Toto, of course. Years later, they would reconnect under far different circumstances. Miller, a war correspondent, was taking photographs of concentration camps that had just been liberated, while Toto had experienced the horror of deportation firsthand.

6

When she was not working, Toto was courted by Parisian café society. Her exotic looks, her lack of inhibition and her open-mindedness made her what Proust defined as a "golden guest" in that cosmopolitan and diverse circle—a group far more accessible than the Faubourg Saint-Germain society crowd, where provenance was a critical factor. Café society favored those who possessed beauty, style, taste, humor, sexual freedom or spectacular fortunes. Any one of these criteria was enough to gain entry; but for the large bank account, Toto had them all.

Choosing those with whom she would or would not spend time was Toto's greatest luxury. Driven by a constant need for stimulation and a cheerful disregard for conventional morality, she sought out only interesting and creative people and, whenever possible, people who had both qualities: bogus Russian princes, couturiers, photographers and wealthy foreigners such as Caresse Crosby and Lady Iya Abdy.

Abdy, a White Russian émigrée, played piano in a movie theater before marrying a British aristocrat; she quickly divorced him but kept his title. For a time, she was Coco Chanel's assistant and accessory designer. She was a "jockey" for Molyneux and a friend of the painters André Derain and Balthus, for whom she posed. But Abdy was mainly known for the soirées she hosted at her Quai de Bourbon and place Vendôme homes, where Toto was a regular guest. One section of her apartment was always locked and off-limits; gossip-mongers whispered that Abdy was keeping her parents, simple Russian peasants, away from prying eyes.

Toto was closer to Caresse Crosby, a young woman from a prominent New York family. Caresse and her second husband, Harry Crosby, formed a charismatic and eccentric couple. They were a living caricature of characters out of an F. Scott Fitzgerald novel, but their narrative went beyond the author's wildest imagination. The Paris-based American couple founded the Black Sun Press and published the works of T.S. Eliot, Ezra Pound and James Joyce. Caresse was also a writer, and T.E. Lawrence, the famous Lawrence of Arabia, was said to be so taken with her poems that he always kept a collection of them at his side. They smuggled gold pieces into Italy to help D.H. Lawrence publish *Lady Chatterley's Lover*. (Did Toto recall this episode years later, when she did something similar for Francis Bacon?)

The Crosbys welcomed their guests from their bed, reprising a 17th-century tradition. Their afghan hound, Black Narcissus, had gold-painted nails and a leash and collar custom made by Cartier. They hosted *mad parties*, inviting the most beautiful women in attendance to join them in their bathtub. Their rue de Lille apartment was famous for its library filled with rare editions and human bones, stolen from the catacombs by the master of the house. Caresse was the inventor of the first modern brassiere to be patented. Harry, a poet, was an opium addict who took his own life in December 1929, at the age of thirty-one.

While Toto was not interested in marriage, children or a permanent residence, she did establish deep and lasting friendships with several women. Besides Nina Mdivani, Lee Miller and Caresse Crosby, her closest friend was another American, Bettina Jones, who at the time was married to the French politician Gaston Bergery. "The beautiful Madame Bergery is probably a clandestine genius inasmuch as she is indecipherable, unintelligible, utterly disconcerting," wrote Violet Trefusis in *Prelude to Misadventure*. "Each of her remarks is a decoy leading her audience astray, as a seemingly wounded bird will deliberately lead the pursuer away from its nest."[6] An apt description of Bettina's desire to be unique, a desire that led to many excesses.

The Jones family was already known for its eccentricity—one of Bettina's sisters lived in an abandoned church—but Bettina gave new meaning to the word. Elsa Schiaparelli, for whom she was both muse and assistant, further encouraged her to live out all her fantasies. The Italian designer was Coco Chanel's rival, and her creations were very influenced by surrealism: suits with bureau drawer pockets—her nod to Dali's *Cabinet Anthropomorphique*; a hat in the shape of a lamb chop; fabric patterned to look as if it were torn; handbags shaped like birdcages or flower pots. Her imagination was limitless and her *trompe l'oeil* creations were technically faultless thanks to the extraordinary ateliers that could meet any challenge she sent their way.

Bettina Jones sported the most daring designs, such as a shocking pink velvet hat in the shape of a shoe. Like Roussy Mdivani, Bettina carried a small monkey with her at all times. The monkey bit anyone who displeased its mistress; in the winter, it wore a little coat designed by Schiaparelli. Armed with perfect features, cutting-edge style and mordant wit, Jones felt invulnerable and fearless. At a garden party in June 1933, Toto witnessed a scene that sent shivers through all the guests—including Salvador Dalí and Jean Cocteau, two men who were hard to shock. Caresse Crosby was hosting a *fête champêtre* at Le Moulin du Soleil, her country home in Ermenonville that was supposedly haunted by the ghost of Cagliostro (the Italian occultist implicated in the Affair of the Diamond Necklace). When Jones saw her husband, Gaston Bergery, being seduced by Marie de Gramont, she crushed her lit cigarette into the duchess's naked shoulder. Such outrageous behavior, paired with her Schiaparelli outfits, perfectly mirrored the surrealist bent that was characteristic of cafe society.

The impetuous American was at her best when designing ingenious window displays for the Schiaparelli *maison de couture* on place Vendôme. These displays became tourist attractions that rivaled the Eiffel Tower and the Arc de Triomphe. Bettina often collaborated with Dalí, who was a close friend and shared her taste for the unusual. One of their projects involved dying a giant teddy bear hot pink—Schiaparelli's signature color—and installing drawers in the teddy bear's stomach that they then filled with jewelry.

Bettina encouraged Toto to borrow her clothes and accessories, and Miss K. happily delved into this bottomless treasure chest. Over the years, Toto wore the creations of the three most important designers of the 1930s: she modeled for Chanel, was photographed in Vionnet for *Vogue* and went about town in Schiaparelli. Always drawn to eccentricity, Toto added quirky accessories, such as gloves with red lizard skin between the fingers, intentionally made to look like diseased skin—definitively Schiaparelli.

In all the years she spent in Paris, Toto had only one French friend. Marcelle Oury worked for couturier Paul Poiret as press agent—a job title that did not exist at the time and that she invented to define her work. She was a close friend of the painters Tsuguharu Foujita and Raoul Dufy. Toto was in awe of Oury's apartment, with its extensive collection of Dufy paintings, and still spoke about it at the end of her life. Marcelle, the mother and grandmother of filmmakers Gérard Oury and Danièle Thompson, respectively, was a loyal friend to Toto, and they continued to see each other regularly after the war.

Though a proud fixture of café society and a willing participant in its frivolity and pleasure, Miss K., who managed to embody the contradictory concepts of insouciance and determination, was not entirely in line with it. Without the benefit of money or lineage, she had worked since the age of nineteen and her independence was achieved on her own terms.

7

In the 1930s, all of Miss K.'s Parisian friends longed to be in the movies, and a few succeeded. Lee Miller appeared in Jean Cocteau's *The Blood of a Poet*, playing the part of a living statue. In 1932, Hoyningen-Huene directed a drama, a film that is lost today, featuring Horst, his assistant and lover, and Natalie Paley, the splendid Romanoff princess whose life's journey could be compared to a trip on board the *Nautilus*, Jules Verne's fictional submarine. Toto was soon seduced as well. The official version has Toto heading to London after learning that director and producer Alexander Korda was holding auditions there for his new film, *The Private Life of Don Juan*. Toto took a screen test and landed the part of one of the famous seducer's mistresses. Natalie Paley was also cast in the film.

"Actually, it was her friend Conrad Veidt who convinced her to sign a contract with Korda," explained

Toto's friend F.C. "Had they met in Germany? In London or Paris? It does not matter, they all traveled extensively. They got along famously and Veidt, whose Nosferatu-like character appealed to Toto, persuaded her to go ahead. He probably thought that Toto, who was so incredibly photogenic, would be perfect for the big screen."

Bitterly opposed to the Nazi regime, the actor had moved to London in 1933 to protect his Jewish wife. At the time, he personified German Expressionism and was known for his roles as a psychopath or a pervert: he played Cesare, the homicidal somnambulist in *The Cabinet of Doctor Caligari* (1920), and Gwynplaine, the disfigured circus artist in *The Man Who Laughs* (1928)—a performance that inspired the part of the Joker in the *Batman* series. Film buffs also remember him as Major Strasser in *Casablanca* (1942). In addition to Veidt, Toto befriended many other artists who had fled the growing Nazi threat.

Miss K. was enchanted at the thought of working for Alexander Korda, whose extravagant style was so typically *Mitteleuropean*. After fleeing the regime of Béla Kun in his native Hungary, young Korda lived in many different cities in the first half of the 1920s before settling down in Hollywood, where he directed sixteen films. But America could never live up to Korda's beloved France or England. "For a time, he lived and worked in Paris before settling in London," remembered Denise Tual, his friend and collaborator.

"A Hungarian Jew from a very poor family, he had an innate taste for luxury and his brilliant sense of business allowed him to live the high life. When I met him, he was living at the Ritz, place Vendôme, and when he moved to a suite at Claridge's, in London, an orchestra played czardas and Viennese waltzes while footmen in full livery wore white gloves to carry his prized paintings. I never forgot that moment. It says more about Alexander than volumes of writing." Indeed, he was a perfect match for Toto.

In London, the ambitious and ruthless businessman—tough and wildly jovial at the same time—founded his own production company in 1932; he called it London Films and chose Big Ben as its logo. With the backing of his brothers Zoltan and Vincent, Alexander could now give in to his penchant for extravagant costume dramas. While *The Private Life of Henry VIII* appealed to a wide audience, the same would not hold true for his next project.

Released on September 10, 1934, *The Private Life of Don Juan* was a stodgy farce starring an aging and heavy-set Douglas Fairbanks. It was set in a picture-perfect Seville replete with predictable balconies ready to be scaled. Only Olivier Messel's superb costumes redeemed the dreary film. The leading lady and Korda's then-current mistress, Merle Oberon, was unconvincing as a flamenco dancer. Miss K. did not appear in the film—all her scenes had been cut during the editing.

"Toto found filming tedious," recalled Lady Deirdre Curteis. "The endless waiting between takes was unbearable. She yearned for action and excitement." Miss K. was not about to give up her modeling career—though she eventually would in 1934—to be imprisoned once again in a static environment. One morning, Toto did not show up on the set and Korda, realizing she would not return, immediately terminated her contract. Still, they remained on the best of terms and saw each other regularly at the home of their friend Moura Budberg.

Many photographs of Toto were taken during the filming and, oddly, those still shots were used to promote the film. She gave many interviews and the press predicted a bright future for her in movies. There was talk of a new project with the actor and director Monty Banks, who had worked with Laurel and Hardy. But none of this came about, as Toto had definitively given up the world of the cinema. However, she did attend the première of *The Private Life of Don Juan* in the company of Tallulah Bankhead and their appearance as a couple caused a sensation.

Miss K. and the American actress were lovers. Tallulah Bankhead was an authentic southern belle whose wild and eccentric lifestyle filled the gossip pages. In 1934 she had not yet appeared in Hitchcock's *Lifeboat*, which would be her biggest critical and commercial success, but her reputation, both on stage and on the screen, was already well established. She appeared regularly on the London stage and the press covered every detail of her escapades, to the delight of the British public.

The stunning flame-haired Bankhead was a friend of F. Scott and Zelda Fitzgerald's and a member of the Algonquin Round Table in New York. She could easily consume one or two bottles of bourbon each day, smoked close to one hundred cigarettes between dawn and dusk and never tired of singing the praises of her hunch-backed cocaine dealer, a black man named Money. "My father warned me about men and booze, but he never said anything about women and cocaine," she responded when asked about her bisexuality. She was thrilled to be implicated in a moral scandal involving fourteen-year-old Eton students. Like Sarah Bernhardt fifty years earlier, she craved the limelight: *Talk about me in good terms or bad, just talk about me.*

Bankhead was worshipped by British lesbians, who watched her every move and manner and followed her everywhere. They gathered by the hundreds to welcome her at train stations. When the actress suddenly decided to cut her long hair herself, they followed her example; at the end of her performances, in lieu of flowers, they tossed handfuls of hair onto the stage.

Toto and Tallulah met in London in 1934. The attraction was mutual and immediate. To outsiders, the two women seemed as strange and fascinating as iridescent underwater creatures armed with venomous stingers. Unpredictable and narcissistic, infatuated with their own originality, they loved to be seen together. They could be as appealing as they were repellent. The liaison was short-lived, lasting only a few months, and was not unlike the relationship Toto had with Alexis Mdivani—a momentary pleasure without commitment. Tallulah Bankhead eventually returned to America, of course, and Toto would always cherish the time they had spent together.

8

In Paris, Toto mingled with talented and witty people, but it was not until she moved to London that she entered the world of the truly powerful. The person who would singlehandedly alter the direction of her life was Lord Beaverbrook, whose mistress she became. When she left France for the British capital, she could never have anticipated that the relationship would ignite such a colossal scandal.

In 1934, when Tallulah Bankhead introduced Toto and William Aitken, by then Lord Beaverbrook, he was fifty-five years old and Toto just twenty-five. Aitken was an omnipotent press baron, the Citizen Kane of London. The brilliant and diminutive billionaire, whose entourage included both courtiers and foes, was immediately attracted to Miss K.'s looks, personality and relaxed sexual attitude. Toto, who aspired to more substance in her daily life, could not help but feel flattered at being pursued and desired by one of the country's most important people. She had developed a serious interest in politics, and Beaverbrook would provide entry into that world; she didn't have a moment's hesitation.

Fight, fight, fight. Never give in. Never say, 'I give up.' Beaverbrook lived by the same credo as French author André Suarès. Like the Mdivanis, he exaggerated the hardships of his early life in order to make his success sound all the more spectacular. He had not walked to school barefoot, as he liked to say. Born in 1879, William Aitken was the son of a Scottish minister who immigrated to Canada. While the family did live in a remote and impoverished area, their home was large and staffed by several servants—hardly the setting of a Dickens novel. There was no running water or electricity, which was the norm at the time, but photographs show that young William wore suits made of velvet, not rags, as he claimed. Still, the large family of ten had limited means, and from a very young age William dreamed of making a fortune.

At sixteen, he quit school, left home and set off to earn a living. Armed with courage, tireless ambition, determination and a keen sense of business, he held several jobs before establishing himself as a prominent insurance agent. His clients included bankers and industrialists who would eventually help him rise socially. His rigorous discipline was his best ally: he worked from dawn to dusk, standing at a lectern and never sitting down. He imposed the same rules on his colleagues, who were also required to stand.

His shrewd investments in steel, cement, electricity and newspapers—he wisely ventured into every sector—made him a wealthy man. In 1910 he left Canada and moved to England where, always seeking a challenge, he acquired the Rolls-Royce automobile company. Passionate about politics, Aitken made many contacts in the Conservative Party. He befriended Rudyard Kipling, author of *The Jungle Book* and the most universally acclaimed British writer of the time and winner of the 1907 Nobel Prize in Literature; always the consummate opportunist, Aitken would make the most of his connection to the famous author.

William Aitken became a member of Parliament at the age of thirty-one, after winning the Lancashire district election—an extraordinary accomplishment for a Canadian. From this point on, he lived and worked in London and his colossal hunger for power enabled him to withstand the humiliation and insults hurled his way. Envious of his success, many cruelly mocked him as a *parvenu*. But he was tenacious, and with the help of his supporters, he was knighted in 1911. Aitken was jubilant. His nomination was challenged by many of his enemies, but Aitken was confident he could overcome all obstacles and succeed thanks to his considerable fortune. He often did.

With exceptional intuition, he recognized the power of the press and how it could support his various projects and undertakings. To this purpose, he acquired the *Daily Express*, the first piece of his future newspaper conglomerate, which would include the *Sunday Express* and the *Evening Standard*. Aitken became Lord Beaverbrook and in February 1918, when he was appointed the wartime minister of information and propaganda, even his harshest critics acknowledged just how far this young Canadian insurance salesman had come.

Winston Churchill found him irritating and called him "Machiavelli"; the writer Evelyn Waugh, who also wrote articles for Beaverbrook's papers, caricatured him in three different books. But Lord Beaverbrook's thirst for power was unquenchable and he was a ubiquitous presence on the British scene: he invested in film companies, bought racehorses and generously supported hospitals and universities. But his greatest power was the ability to make or break someone's reputation through his newspapers.

Privately, he was the complete opposite of a triumphant and predatory capitalist: Beaverbrook was a hypochondriac who suffered from paranoia; he was anxious and often depressed. Unattractive and squat—a friend once compared the shape of his body to a pair of scissors—with a face covered in warts, he played the role of Quasimodo to Europe and America's most beautiful Esmeraldas. Desirable women everywhere welcomed his advances, especially after he became a widower in 1927. On the international scene, Beaverbrook was a great catch.

But power and money do not explain everything. Indeed, he led a life of luxury and his entourage benefited from his generosity—evenings at the Savoy, weekends in his country houses, cruises. Just as Aristotle Onassis would years later, Beaverbrook knew how to draw attention away from his physique with an irresistible mix of energy, wit, humor and generosity—a selective generosity, of course. Conversations around his dinner table were scintillating, and banality nonexistent. No Adonis could outshine him.

Toto was the perfect antidote to Beaverbrook's only true enemy, boredom. Like many others, he found her beauty and sexual energy disconcerting, but he was attracted to her independent spirit and impulsive nature. She was proud and free and unpredictable, with a sense of curiosity that matched his own.

Beaverbrook was caught up in his self-made web of highly compensated sycophants who catered to all his whims without ever contradicting him. Many fought to remain in his favor, but Toto was not among them. She was unfailingly straightforward, never seeking to flatter or ingratiate herself. Her attitude intrigued and seduced the powerful fifty-five-year-old. Toto became his mistress with her head held high, believing theirs was an even exchange.

9

The jungle of conspirators and social climbers that formed the Beaverbrook circle could aptly be described by a Chinese proverb: "Gold and jade on the outside, rot and decay on the inside." One had to enjoy swimming in dangerous waters to survive in this world of manipulation and deceit. Toto, who always preferred chaos to quiet, showed a remarkable facility for adapting to this new milieu. She watched with amusement as politicians and artists shamelessly courted her lover to win the support of his newspapers. More importantly, she finally became aware of the brutality and rancor that permeated the 1930s.

Beaverbrook and Moura Budberg were Toto's political mentors. A renowned hostess, Baroness Budberg had been the mistress of both Maxim Gorky, the author of Soviet social literature, and H.G. Wells. In her London salon, writers, diplomats and journalists mingled with stars of the stage and screen. Alexander Korda was among them and Budberg often selected screenplays for him. Was Budberg really a double agent, working for both the Soviets and the British? Many thought so, but she kept everyone guessing. The more fanciful among them spoke of a direct lineage to Peter the Great: that her forefather, Count Zakrevsky, was a secret son of Empress Elizabeth. When Alexander Korda introduced them, Miss K. was immediately captivated by Budberg's intriguing background.

Beaverbrook and Budberg were consumed with politics, as were their friends. They spent hours discussing the future of Europe, especially after Adolf Hitler was named chancellor in January 1933. Through them, Toto met Robert Vansittart and Stewart Menzies, the éminences grises of British government. Vansittart, a close friend of Alexander Korda's and a cousin to Lawrence of Arabia, was a skilled politician and the permanent under-secretary of the foreign office from 1930 to 1938. Stewart Menzies was chief of British secret intelligence service for thirteen years and the inspiration for "M," James Bond's superior in the novels of Ian Fleming. Toto was therefore privy to the most incisive and nuanced analyses of political issues, along with first-hand knowledge of the latest developments. She listened avidly and later would set off to see for herself what was actually taking place on the continent.

When Air France was founded in 1933, Toto, already nomadic in spirit, was quick to embrace an easier form of travel. Our nymph Europa was afflicted by "itchy wings." Her passion for opera was one of the things that led her from venue to venue, from Covent Garden to La Scala. Fluent in many languages, she easily made her way around the world.

Toto's travel presented an opportunity for Beaverbrook. His paranoia knew no bounds and he had spies follow his wife, children and friends. He lived by the divide-and-conquer philosophy. Reports were brought to him concerning every move of celebrities and commoners, as nobody escaped his appetite for indiscretion and his taste for blackmail. He ran his newspaper empire with the same mindset: news was based on scoops and insatiable curiosity and he had to be the first to know everything. According to those close to Toto, he had asked his young mistress to gather information during her frequent trips to Germany and Italy.

Miss K. did seem perfectly suited to the role. Multilingual, naturally curious and fascinated by the behind-the-scene strategies of international politics, she had been traveling throughout Europe for years to attend every season's musical performances. Too visible to arouse suspicion or concern, she easily passed under the radar of embassies and border controls. Toto was worldly and knew many people who could be useful, and Beaverbrook, cynic that he was, knew Toto would use sex as a means to justify the end.

From Berlin to Rome, from Milan to Salzburg and from Venice to Bayreuth, Toto went about harvesting information. Between operas, she listened, blithely asking questions, circulating through Hitler's Germany and Mussolini's Italy on behalf of her Anglo-Canadian press baron. She met people whose names appeared in the headlines; she flirted and established contacts. She had a brief affair with Herbert von Karajan, who had just joined the Nazi Party. "Everyone believed she was the mistress of Mussolini's son-in-law, Count Ciano," remembered Toto's friend Gianna Sistu. Sistu was not the only one of Toto's close friends to mention her presumed relationship with Ciano.

While there is definite evidence of her espionage activities during World War II, her movements in 1935 remain unverifiable. Perhaps the biggest question surrounds whether she was involved in meetings Beaverbrook held that year with Mussolini and Hitler.

Although he was a staunch opponent of anti-Semitism, in November 1935 Beaverbrook went to meet Hitler and visit the German military installations, just as he had gone to Rome several months earlier to meet Mussolini. He had at his disposal his own plane, manned by the Swiss pilot Walter Mittleholzer, who served as intermediary between the press baron and the German authorities. Unlike Toto, who was fluent in both languages, Beaverbrook spoke neither German nor Italian. Did Toto travel with him as his interpreter when he met with Mussolini and Hitler? Many have wondered, but nobody can say for sure, even though the idea that she could have been present at such an exclusive meeting is intriguing.

By late 1935, however, the relationship between Miss K. and Lord B. had rapidly deteriorated. After having pursued her with such determination, Beaverbrook would ultimately do everything in his power to destroy her reputation.

10

Unbeknownst to Beaverbrook, Toto had been having an affair with his son, Max Aitken. When Beaverbrook learned that Toto and Max had been seen out and about in London, his outrage was immeasurable. To make matters worse, this relationship was more than a fling—young Max was said to be hopelessly in love. Furthermore, Lord B. learned that his best friend, the Viscount Castlerosse, was also in love with Miss K., Viscountess Castlerosse was threatening to sue her husband for divorce and name Toto as co-defendant. Through it all, Toto remained unperturbed, paying no attention to the ongoing uproar. She was in love, and nothing else mattered.

When Max proposed marriage, his father immediately tried to get rid of Toto. Miss K. burst out laughing when she learned that Lord B. called her "that negress," referring to her background. It would take more than that to rattle her, however, and the mediocrity of his insult left her unruffled. The old lion decided to sully her reputation and make her disappear. He barred his newspapers from mentioning the name of "the culprit" and began a defamation campaign against her in London society that was particularly vicious. It was time for the branding iron and the scarlet letter.

For Beaverbrook, Toto's name was now synonymous with sin and lust. There was no small irony to be found in these accusations coming from someone who was not particularly innocent himself. Indeed, Toto's only wrongdoing was behaving like a man. Her insolence, her defiance of conventions and complete lack of taboos and sexual hypocrisy—she drifted casually from the arms of a man to those of a woman, from the bed of the father to that of the son—would send shockwaves through the self-righteous people of England in the 1930s. Lord B. intended to use that fact to his best advantage.

Such attacks only reinforced Toto's determination to live life as she pleased. Never had the Koopman sorceress been more beautiful, more determined or more dangerously free. People were mesmerized by her, their feelings caught between fascination and horror. She scoffed at being a social outcast and troublemaker, fearing neither insults nor blackmail. Toto felt no shame, nor was she concerned about maintaining her social position. Her determination made it possible for her to withstand the most hurtful and spiteful remarks.

Her lifestyle was a tribute to moral freedom and reminiscent of that of Ninon de Lenclos, another scandalous courtesan who humorously classified her lovers into three categories: the payers, the martyrs and the favorites. Father and son Beaverbrook belonged, respectively, to the first and third categories. Lord Castlerosse belonged to the second group: portly, bald, religious and born to suffer, he repeatedly fell for *femmes fatales*, Miss K. included, who thought of him only as an amusing companion. He was the perfect martyr.

At twenty-seven, Toto resolutely held her own against the old lion. Many people shunned her, fearing the wrath of Britain's most powerful press baron. She was on her own. Her Parisian friends were far away, and she had not seen her family for a long time. Her mother had died in July 1933 and Toto chose not to visit her on her deathbed but rather to remember her as she was. Her father left the army to become a director of the Royal Dutch Airlines and her brother, Ody, was now a banker in Holland. The two men led quiet lives, far from the chaos that engulfed Toto.

When Lord Beaverbrook realized that his tactics were not succeeding, he turned on Max, who was still determined to marry Toto. Beaverbrook *père* threatened to cut off and disinherit his son. That approach failed as well, resulting in a vicious animosity between the two men, where jealousy mixed with racism.

As was his way, Beaverbrook spied on them day and night. The couple managed to escape to Spain for a time, where they stayed with Roussy and José Maria Sert. When they returned, Lord B. resumed his harassment. Toto did not speak about this episode for many years. However, a few months before her death, she agreed to meet with Anne Chisholm, the author of a biography of Beaverbrook, to reveal both her feelings about the man and her side of the story.

Comparing her former lover to "a little monkey," Miss K. described an unattractive man who "had great charm, but he was not lovable, and he wasn't really sure of himself."[7] Chisholm recalled that Toto, who was eighty years old when they met, remained very discreet and chose not to dwell on the subject. She did, however, reveal the negotiations that had occurred over her. "He told Max: 'I'll give you a lot of money if you promise not to marry that girl.' I said, 'Take it!' So he did, and we had a wonderful time."[8] Miss K. did not, however, mention that Beaverbrook offered her a lifetime pension in exchange for the promise that she would never become his daughter-in-law. Believing that he owed her that much, Toto signed the contract.

11

No two men were more fundamentally dissimilar, even diametrically opposite, than Lord Beaverbrook and his son. A year younger than Toto, Max Aitken was born on February 15, 1910. A remarkably gifted athlete, he excelled at all sports, including golf, cricket, soccer and automobile racing. He was also an aviator, having joined the Royal Air Force as an auxiliary pilot in 1935, the year he met Toto. He earned a degree from Cambridge but did not share his father's intellectual curiosity. Unlike his father, he was extremely handsome—it was said that no woman could resist his playboy charms. While the son had more attractive physical attributes, he lacked the depth and resolve of his famous father.

Toto and Max spent the four years following the scandal living in a luxurious penthouse on Portman Square. Their unmarried status was shocking, but they didn't care. Lord B. had relented somewhat in his opposition to the couple's relationship, now that he was certain no official union would take place between them. Sharing a home with a man she loved was a new experience for Toto and it sharpened her natural curiosity. They were both interested in travel and politics—Max would become a member of Parliament after the war—and shared a deep sensual bond.

Free of financial constraints, the couple lived in style. Once the scandal had subsided, they were very sought after by London society. They were seen together everywhere, attending concerts conducted by Sir Thomas Beecham or at the Belgrave Square residence of Henry "Chips" Channon, a wealthy American whose guests included politicians, artists and socialites. His reception room was an astonishing and exact replica of the baroque hall of the Amalienburg Pavilion in Munich—a rococo folly in shades of silver and blue-gray in the very heart of the British capital. One just had to remember not to invite both Beaverbrooks—father and son—on the same night.

Miss K. and her circle of friends lived in a London that was the complete opposite of the rough, industrial, working-class London of Charles Dickens. But the slums described in *David Copperfield* still existed, as very little had changed since the reign of Queen Victoria. London was a city where immutably picturesque facades—bowler hats, imperial red buses, uni-formed governesses looking after children wearing little white gloves—masked the cruel reality of privilege and injustice.

London was also the home of the monarchy and fol-lowed the Buckingham Palace schedule. Toto and Max fell in love during the silver jubilee of King George V and Queen Mary in 1935. Debutantes, coiffed with the obligatory three feathers, were presented each year to the royal couple in a *de rigueur* tribal ritual. Following her 1934 wedding to the Duke of Kent, the beautiful Princess Marina, Duchess of Kent, became the arbiter of fashion for the entire country. No actress was more imitated than she. The notion that the entire country was reeling after the abdication in late 1936 of Edward VIII, the future Duke of Windsor—who chose instead to wed the American divorcée Wallis Simpson—was not an exaggeration. Both the elite and the commoners were quickly consoled by the new coronation.

Toto would always love London. She lived there for the greater part of her life and it was where she spent her final days. While Hitler and Mussolini attempted to transform Europe, and while Europe suffered the consequences of the American economic crash of 1929, Londoners like Miss K. moved about in taxis with meticulously whitewashed tires and lived in lovely stucco homes. At the Covent Garden opera, pro-grams were not distributed by young usherettes but by gentlemen in full eveningwear. Every morning, conscientious milkmen deposited bottles in front of every door. Women rode sidesaddle through Hyde Park, and shoe-shiners still dressed in distinctive red clothing.

Despite their affection for each other, Toto and Max had not given up their sexual freedom. While they lived together, they continued to have affairs with other people. In her biography of Lord Beaverbrook, Anne Chisholm reveals a very telling episode of their *modus vivendi*. When Max's sister, Janet, married William Drogo Montagu, the youngest son of the Earl of Sandwich, Toto and Max accompanied them on their honeymoon in Switzerland. One day, the two men disappeared and were eventually found by Toto and Janet in the company of two other women. Toto had an affair with Randolph Churchill, Winston Churchill's son and one of Max's best friends, yet it had no adverse effect on their relationship.

Exceptionally handsome and intelligent, Randolph Churchill was known for his arrogance and bad temper. Like Max, Randolph Churchill lived in the shadow of his famous father. Though he became an alcoholic at a very young age, he was a very well-respected journalist who wrote brilliant pieces for Lord Beaverbrook's papers in the late 1920s. In 1935, Randolph decided to follow his father's example and enter politics, but he never lived up to his own expectations.

He was bitterly disappointed and often very aggressive. Waiters in some of London's most elegant restaurants bribed their braver colleagues to wait on him. When Randolph was operated on for a benign tumor, Evelyn Waugh, with typical cynicism, declared that the doctors had removed the only part of his body that was not malignant.

Toto fell for this handsome Apollo who loved poetry and could recite hundreds of verses to her at any given moment. Fortunately, she was never subjected to his terrible mood swings. They remained close even after their relationship ended, and Randolph would be the first to come to her aid when she was released from the concentration camp. Miss K. would never forget his support during that tragic time and no one ever dared utter a bad word about him in her presence.

"Toto had affairs, at the same time, with the sons of the two most important men in Great Britain, and that is hardly insignificant," recounted Toto's British friend F.C. "Indeed, they were both intelligent, seductive and committed, but the explanation seems more complex. Max and Randolph never achieved the success of their respective fathers, and we know that it caused them great humiliation. Toto, who had often been scorned, understood their distress and the unfairness of the situation." Theirs was a complicity of misfits.

12

With London as their home base, Toto and Max continued to travel throughout Europe together and separately, and 1936 offered a particularly striking backdrop for their journeys. Instinctively drawn to intriguing people and places, Toto set out for the capitals where history was unfolding.

Toto was in Paris in the spring of 1936 after the Front Populaire emerged victorious in the May elections. France was now governed by a coalition of left-wing parties led by newly elected prime minister Léon Blum. While the country's elite feared the new political situation, Toto's friends continued to make light of things in their own witty and provocative ways.

Bettina Jones Bergery was seen wearing a Schiaparelli dress made of fabric that resembled a patchwork of newspapers, a trompe l'oeil pattern that gave an ironic nod to the latest style worn by the "new poor." The expression *"snobisme de purée,"* a type of reverse snobbery, stigmatized the rich, who hesitated to display their wealth for fear of attracting the attention of "the reds." They were convinced that those who supported the forty-hour workweek and paid holidays were out to get them.

Miss K.'s friendships were always intense and selective. And Hui-Lan Wellington-Koo was a larger than life figure even by Toto's standards. Married to the Chinese ambassador to France, she had all the qualities needed to pique Toto's interest. Having successively navigated the milieus of fashion, café society, film, Fleet Street and politics, Toto was ready to discover the world of diplomacy.

Nina Mdivani introduced them. The British painter Francis Rose described Hui-Lan Wellington-Koo as the most beautiful woman in the world, adding that her beauty was matched only by her keen intelligence. Indeed, she was so bright that it was widely acknowledged that she served as éminence grise to her husband. Mdivani was convinced that her two friends would have much in common.

Both Toto and Hui-Lan Wellington-Koo, who was nine years older than Toto, were born on the island of Java and had to contend with and overcome hostility from the Dutch occupiers. Even though Hui-Lan's father, whom Toto encountered regularly during her childhood, was the richest man in Southeast Asia, the young Chinese woman was subject to racism and contempt from the Dutch. She vowed that nobody would ever humiliate her again.

Like Toto, Wellington-Koo was fluent in several languages. With an innate ability to handle the most delicate situations, she quickly became known for her superb style and became a celebrity in her own right. As the wife of the most brilliant Asian politician of his generation, she was one of the three most famous Chinese women of the time, along with two of the Soong sisters—Madame Chiang Kai-shek and Madame Sun Yat-sen.

Ambassador and Mrs. Wellington arrived in Paris in early 1936 and faced the challenge of representing their country as the world's fifth global power after France, England, Russia and the United States. A graduate of Columbia and Yale, the ambassador was a master at manipulation—in other words, the quintessential diplomat. Still, he recognized his limitations and knew his wife could play an important role at his side.

Hui-Lan immediately captivated Paris society. She was a spectacular hostess and brought a new sense of refinement and sophistication to the avenue Georges-V embassy. Invitations to dinners at the embassy were highly prized. The chef, who had come all the way from Beijing, prepared exotic fare, such as bird's nest and shark's fin soup. At the table, the name of each guest was displayed in a gold place-card holder in the shape of either a dragon or a phoenix—one for the men, the other for the women. These place-card holders often disappeared, as guests slipped them into their pockets as souvenirs; Hui-Lan accepted the fact that she would have to keep replacing them.

She was her father's favorite child, and his seemingly endless money guaranteed her luxurious existence. The ambassador was keenly aware of the impact his wife's glamorous lifestyle had on those around him. Her Rolls-Royce was built to her exact specifications and the chauffeur wore a uniform created by Dunhill of London. Her dresses were made to order by the top Parisian couturiers, using the finest Chinese silks, and she adorned them with priceless jade jewelry. Always accompanied by a pack of Pekingese dogs, she turned heads all over town while mad rumors of all kinds circulated about her.

Many believed that when the Wellington-Koos lived in Beijing, Hui-Lan had taken many young lovers, only to have them beheaded when she grew bored with them. These rumors made her laugh. On the other hand, she really had spent many nights playing poker with Chinese warlords who were as rich as they were cruel. She was the only woman among these bloodthirsty men, and they wagered up to $50,000 at a sitting.

Toto and Hui-Lan shared many of the same interests, most notably their belief in the occult. Their Javanese childhoods had left their mark, and they regularly consulted card readers and astrologers. Hui-Lan was a firm believer in spells and demons and often recounted that her aunt had seen one of her servants turned into a tiger, the Javanese equivalent of a werewolf. In Beijing, she consulted eunuch faith healers and lived in a palace haunted by ghost foxes that were, she believed, a sign of good luck. Toto's story about the sacred javelin was perfectly in line with Hui-Lan's beliefs.

The two women also shared a fascination with politics. Hui-Lan held a great deal of influence over her husband: at the start of the Second Sino-Japanese War in 1937, the American government secretly contacted her and not her ambassador husband to discuss its position on the conflict. Hui-Lan was very close to William Bullitt, the American ambassador to France, who had also taken his position in Paris in 1936.

A writer and diplomat, Bullitt could have been a character created by French writer Paul Morand: Bullitt was psychoanalyzed by Freud during the 1920s in Vienna—they became friends and wrote a book together—and was the first American ambassador appointed to the Soviet Union in 1933. A close friend of President Franklin D. Roosevelt, with whom he spoke daily by telephone, Bullitt was staunchly opposed to communism, as were Hui-Lan and Toto.

Toto, Hui-Lan and Nina Mdivani spent many weekends at the château Bullitt rented in Chantilly, a place reputed to have a cellar of more than 20,000 bottles of grand cru wines. Hui-Lan, an open supporter of the United States, was despised by Mao Tse-tung, one of the founders of the Chinese Communist Party in 1921. When he assumed control of the party in 1935, Mao took his revenge, confiscating all of her possessions, including ten houses, and revoking her Chinese nationality, thus banishing her forever.

13

In the summer of 1936, Toto attended the Olympic Games in Berlin. Her photographs appeared in the society pages of magazines covering the event, but these festive images were not an accurate reflection of her life. Following months of unusually violent conflict, Lord Beaverbrook and Max had ultimately reconciled, and Max accompanied his father to Berlin. Joachim von Ribbentrop, the newly appointed German ambassador to Britain, had personally invited Lord Beaverbrook to attend the games. Beaverbrook and his entourage traveled to Berlin aboard his private plane and attended the opening ceremonies, which were covered at length in his newspapers. If Max was forgiven, Toto remained *persona non grata*. Unfazed, she went to Berlin on her own to witness the events for herself. One wonders whether she was disturbed that Max had capitulated so quickly to his father's wishes.

Miss K. knew Berlin well, having visited regularly since the early 1930s. She was a frequent guest at the Adlon Hotel and intuitively knew her way around the city. Before 1934, she could sense the mood of the city within seconds of setting foot in the Romanische Café. Sophisticated patrons, greeted at the door by a dwarf dressed in uniform, would come to hear Roda, Germany's version of Edith Piaf, sing heartbreaking songs that were mostly declarations of unrequited love to nuns. Writers, actors and painters, as well as the simply curious, found it a refuge of sorts from the raging fury of Nazism. Following the Night of the Long Knives in June 1934 and raids by the SS, who smashed the furniture and attacked those they considered decadent or subversive, the café eventually shut down.

In 1936, Berlin felt like the epicenter of the world. All eyes were on Hitler and his vision of a new Germany. Arms factories were operating at full capacity; the working and middle classes were content, as was the military. In fact, the majority of Berliners had been supporting the Nazi party since 1934.

No expense was spared in planning the Olympic Games. Germany would be seen as a young and triumphant nation but the ceremonies and sporting events filmed with such passion by Leni Riefenstahl and portrayed in *Olympia* could not fully conceal the underlying realities: censored performances and newspapers, widespread book burning of works considered anti-Germanic and radio stations spewing vicious anti-Semitism from morning to night.

Upon her return to Britain, Miss K. was zealous in her support of German friends who had fled Nazism and come to London—among them, Conrad Veidt and the painter Joseph Oppenheimer. She had posed for the latter in the early 1930s. Known for his portraits—of Albert Einstein and Yehudi Menuhin among others—Oppenheimer was a member of the Impressionist secession movement who, like many other persecuted Jewish artists, had fled his native country.

Toto sat for him again in 1938, when she turned thirty, the same year Hitler claimed the adjacent territories of Czechoslovakia after annexing Austria that March. In a portrait that accurately conveys its subject's personality, Oppenheimer depicts a beautiful and stylish woman whose attitude is both disdainful and curious, proudly detached and slightly reticent.

This painting still exists but another portrait of Toto from around that time, by German Jewish artist Max Beckmann, unfortunately does not. Today, Beckmann is considered one of the most important figures of 20th century art, but the Nazis classified him as a "degenerate artist." It is unknown whether Toto posed for him in Berlin or in Amsterdam, where he had sought refuge with his wife. "She spoke about this portrait one day when I mentioned that I knew a collector of Max Beckmann's work. But with her customary discretion, she did not dwell on the subject," recalls Malitte Matta, wife of Chilean artist Roberto Matta. Toto confided to others that Lord Beaverbrook had bought the painting and burned it as an act of revenge. Obsessed with the brutality of the times, Max Beckmann's work is haunted by war and death. The loss of a portrait that could have revealed Toto's personality from a unique perspective is indeed regrettable.

In 1939, after four years together, Toto and Max chose to go their separate ways. More traditionally oriented, Max wanted to settle down and have a family. He was ready to face his father's wrath in order to marry Toto, but she turned him down, knowing that she was not prepared for the role of wife.

For Toto, true freedom was both intellectual and territorial. Her independence was her most treasured possession and she guarded it fiercely. She could not envisage marriage or motherhood for herself, and while many of her contemporaries—including those famous for their libertine ways, such as Vita Sackville-West, Violet Trefusis, Nancy Cunard, Lee Miller and Annemarie Schwarzenbach—eventually wed, Toto never did; the prospect seemed too depressing. Max eventually married Cynthia Monteith, a suitable debutante, and Toto set off towards new adventures just as World War II was about to begin.

14

Toto was in Italy on September 1, 1939, when Nazi troops invaded Poland. Her two adopted countries, France and Britain, responded by declaring war on Germany that same month. That year also marked the start of the underground activities that would thrust her into a period of chaos she could never have foreseen.

Several months later, when Mussolini entered the conflict on the side of the Third Reich, Toto was living in a hotel in Florence. All we know about that time is that she had left both Max and London to meet up with Hungarian friends who were wealthy art collectors. "That was when she fell in love with a leader of the Italian Resistance," added F.C. The circumstances under which she would have met such a man remain unknown to her friend, but F.C. reported, "Toto sold her furs and jewelry to provide financial support for him and his partisans. She spied for them and also for the Allies, at Max Aitken's request, as they had remained close."

This fact was confirmed by Elisabeth Eichmann, a young German woman Toto met at that time who would become one of her closest friends. "My sister Ingerborg and I had obtained authorization to pursue our studies in Italy, which enabled us to escape from the hell that was ravaging our country," remembered Eichmann, now in her nineties. "Toto and I were soul mates from the minute we met. I adored her, she was so special and determined, unique in every way. I was much more reserved and shy. She had a way of seeing the light in the midst of a storm. Her combination of strength and humor was surprisingly reassuring during this very stressful time. Toto knew she could trust me implicitly. She asked me to go with her to a Fascist meeting, where we would pretend to be sympathizers. The Black Shirts had no idea she was taking mental notes in order to write a report for the Italian Resistance and the British government."

How did Toto pass on her reports? Did she turn them over to liaison officers? And who was reading these reports? "I haven't the slightest idea and I never dared to ask the question, even years later," Eichmann said. "As for the Resistance leader with whom she fell in love, I met him but I forget his name. It was so long ago. I was amazed by Toto's courage. She exhibited remarkable *sang-froid* and risked everything to stand up for her convictions."

Clichés abound when it comes to female spies: it would be easy to think of Miss K. as a combination of Mata Hari and Christine Keeler or as a real-life version of a gorgeous James Bond girl. But Toto's story is a far more sober one and her romantic involvement with a member of the Resistance went hand in hand with her strong ethical and political convictions. According to writer and journalist William Rospigliosi, who was held in captivity alongside her, Toto had become an intelligence agent for the Italian Resistance as well as for the British—because of her ideological convictions, she wanted to help the Allies. She made the decision without a moment's hesitation.

Toto had the requisite talents to be an undercover operative. With no close family ties, an independent spirit and a remarkable ability to adapt to new circumstances, as well as an uncanny gift for observation and her attraction to unusual people, she could survive in the most hostile of environments. Guided by instinct, she was confident that she could always make the best of any difficult situation. Long accustomed to intrigue, Miss K. knew how to deal with adversaries and danger.

Elisabeth Eichmann's testimony confirmed that Toto knew how to size up her enemies.

But it would not last long. The Italian police arrested her in January 1941. "Toto ran out of luck," said her friend Edmonde Charles-Roux. "She had highly-placed contacts in Italy; I know for a fact that she was received by Isabelle Colonna, and one did not gain entry to the princess's circle without having very solid contacts. Toto was very connected, but someone must have really had it in for her to have kept her locked in prison for so many years."

In a letter to Elisabeth Eichmann dated December 20, 1945, shortly after her release from the camps, Miss K. gave her own version of the facts: "I was arrested (by the Fascists) under the old pretext of being... Beaverbrook's mistress. But once I was in jail, ... what they wanted was to free me and I was to do some terribly dirty work. I am so curious, was there some plot or something going on in Italy?... Of course, I refused flatly.... The partisans helped us no ends [sic] but they couldn't possibly let me free after all the things they had told me."

Following her arrest, Toto was taken to Milan's San Vittore Prison. The winter of 1941 was especially harsh, and the wind blew directly into Toto's unheated cell through a broken windowpane. Toto, who suffered intensely from the cold and humidity, slept in her clothes on a straw mattress with two rough wool blankets. The room contained a table, a basin of cold water for washing up and, in the corner, an odd wood contraption that served as a toilet.

She was given very little to eat and the guards taunted the beautiful stranger they believed to be a spy. They snickered as they tried to catch her in her most intimate moments. "Toto always said that the Italians were far from the charming and endearing people they were reputed to be. She suffered terrible humiliation at their hands," recalled Lady Deirdre Curteis. During her imprisonment in San Vittore, Miss K. spent hours dancing the Charleston in an attempt to ward off the cold.

After two months, she was transferred to a detention camp in Bolsena, near Viterbo. Italian author and journalist William Rospigliosi, also arrested for his anti-Fascist stance, gave the following detailed description of the nightmare she suffered:

> The conditions of detention in Bolsena were
> particularly appalling and, furthermore, some
> of the local inhabitants who objected to the
> presence of what they called "an enemy of Italy
> and Germany" in their village put pressure
> on the Italian authorities. Miss Koopman was
> therefore sent to another detention camp . . .
> in the same area. It was only after one year's
> imprisonment that Miss Koopman was moved
> to a detention camp in Perugia that was con-
> sidered more humane.[9]

Many wild rumors circulated about Toto during her lifetime but one of the most laughable was linked to this time period. In a memoir[10] published in 1999, John Richardson, art historian and biographer of Picasso, claimed that Toto—"a seductive, partly Javanese adventuress"—had become the mistress of the camp's commandant, who thus offered to release her; she accepted only on the condition that her friends and fellow prisoners Elisabeth and Ingerborg Eichmann would also be released. The commandant agreed and Miss K. saved her friends.

"But my sister and I were never prisoners in a camp!" exclaimed Elisabeth Eichmann. "I have heard this crazy story before. Toto had the capacity to inflame people's imaginations, in spite of herself. It is true that I was in Perugia at the same time, but only to pursue my studies. Prisoners were allowed to receive visitors and could even walk around a restricted area, so I did see Toto quite often. And I can assure you that she was not the mistress of the commandant!" When asked about this, John Richardson did not conceal his surprise. "I really believed, in good faith, that it was true because I had heard this story several times."

According to William Rospigliosi, who was also held in Perugia, Toto's very presence was a source of tension. "Here again, the local people, those who supported Germany and Mussolini, directed their animosity toward Miss Koopman—accusing her of being a great enemy of the Axis. Consequently, in the spring of 1943, she was sent to the Massa Martana detention camp near Terni."

15

On July 25, 1943, Mussolini was overthrown and arrested on the orders of King Victor Emmanuel III. There was tremendous confusion throughout the country. Many political prisoners were freed that summer, but Toto was not among them. "She was not immediately liberated," wrote William Rospigliosi. "On her own, she managed to take refuge in the mountains where, in any way she could, she helped and financed a group of former prisoners who were part of the Allied forces. Other war prisoners soon joined them. I was able to flee Perugia thanks to a network that was put in place by Miss Koopman to help those who wanted to escape the Germans."

Over the years, Toto revealed various facts to different people about her activities during this period. She recounted her escape from the Massa Martana camp just as the Fascists were about to send the prisoners to Germany; she described her time living in the mountains, where she was the only woman among two hundred and fifty men. Toto slept outside, on the ground, under a blanket. She could wash herself only in cold water and only did so after the men were asleep, as she was reluctant to undress in front of them.

After several weeks of spartan existence and worn down by two and a half years of imprisonment, Miss K. quietly moved to a small village down the mountain that had been deserted temporarily by the enemy. The farmers there welcomed her warmly, and she regained some of her strength. She continued to inform members of the Resistance about the activities she witnessed in the valley; Mussolini's supporters had regained some ground in the interim. She also helped several prisoners of war make their way to southern Italy.

She had gained the trust of the local people and they, in turn, would direct any fugitives they encountered her way. Toto provided them with shelter, served as translator for British paratroopers and supplied them with food and roughly drawn maps before they moved on. She kept all the thank-you notes she received from those she helped and hid them for a time in the house of a local woman she had befriended.

This was Toto's routine for several months, until a Sicilian tried to steal some trucks that the Resistance members were hiding in the woods. He was caught in the act and punished severely. The traitor took his revenge by reporting the group to the Perugian Fascist authorities. Miss K. and the others were arrested during a surprise raid in the middle of the night. Toto was locked up in the cell of a local jail, a tiny damp windowless room furnished with only a wood bench.

A few hours later, at dawn, she heard several vehicles pull up. Several men yelled out, "Where is the spy?" Inebriated Black Shirts began insulting her and ordered her to get up. Only when threatened with a gun did she comply. "Get her outside and let's have some fun with her!" they shouted. Years later, Toto still remembered how afraid she was of being gang-raped and how death seemed a better alternative.

The villagers—including the Carabinieri, who had taken a liking to her, played poker with her in the evenings and looked the other way regarding her activities in the Resistance—were dismayed, but none had the nerve to stand up to the armed Black Shirts. Toto was saved by the arrival of an officer, who ordered them to stop by shooting his gun into the air. "She's the British one, the spy," they shouted. "Leave her alone and get out," he replied. They obeyed reluctantly, and Toto found herself alone with the blond blue-eyed man, who was clearly not Italian. "I apologize, the boys are very agitated because we are about to entrap members of the Resistance and there will undoubtedly be some violent fighting," he said. A few moments later, the stranger whispered, "I am one of yours. I am British. I am part of the secret intelligence service."

Although she was exhausted from lack of sleep and raw nerves, she did not give in to his siren song. "I don't care if you do or don't belong to the secret intelligence service. For pity's sake, get me out of here," she answered. The officer promised he would, then left. Miss K. wondered whether he really was British. And if he was not, why pretend to be? Would he really help her escape?

When he returned, the stranger asked Toto to kiss him. She remembered wanting to slap him in anger. "You're no better than the others. Get me out of here first, then I'll think about it." The man apologized for his boorishness and promised to get her out before vanishing once again. Her suspicions were confirmed when one of the Carabinieri revealed that the man was on the best of terms with high-placed Fascists; Toto was already apprehensive, and this information only added to her torment.

The wait seemed endless, and Toto could hear the sounds of fighting in the distance. She had no way of knowing whether her companions had survived the attack. The daughter of the town innkeeper, who brought Toto food, announced that the leader of their group had been killed. Toto was shattered. Later that day, the blond officer returned, accompanied by two Black Shirts. He offered to drive her to the Hotel Italia in Perugia, where she would be more comfortable than in the sordid cell. Toto no longer knew what to believe, but she accepted his offer. She soon discovered that the hotel had been converted into a prison. Guards were stationed inside as well as outside, and she was not allowed to leave her room. The detainees were allowed to gather for one hour each day on a small terrace.

Toto spent weeks at the hotel, and the endless waiting left her frail and vulnerable. All her hopes rested on the advance of the Allies, but the rumors circulating among the prisoners were so contradictory that it was impossible to understand what was really happening. One afternoon, Toto answered a knock on her door and found a handsome Italian man in a paratrooper's uniform waiting to see her. After the customary salute, he asked for her help. He also claimed to belong to the secret intelligence service and explained that he had just arrived from Rome to track down a dangerous anti-Fascist and his Greek mistress. The Perugian authorities had directed him to Toto, as she was supposedly well acquainted with all the foreigners in the area.

Toto studied the photograph the Italian man showed her and told him that she knew nothing about the man in question. Now that she was aware of the enemy's methods, she was on her guard. Did they really think she could be fooled so easily? She decided to cajole him, and within the hour she had gained the upper hand. He then revealed all the details of his mission.

Toto learned that the blond blue-eyed officer— born in England to a Norwegian mother and an Italian father—was a rabid Fascist. His job was to uncover spies who were collaborating with the Allies, and he went about it with rare zeal. In the hopes of uncovering some information about her friends in the Resistance, he had pretended to save her life when the Black Shirts threatened her. Having failed to draw anything out of her that way, he'd sent this handsome young man, an actor, disguised as a paratrooper.

Soon after this incident, Miss K. was able to escape with the help of the Resistance.

"Toto managed to reach Venice, where I was staying and we were so happy to see each other," Elisabeth Eichmann remembered. "A friend, whose name I have unfortunately forgotten, offered to hide her in the Hotel Danieli, where she was living." Miss K. often recounted this story. "That friend learned that the Hotel Danieli was going to be searched that very night from top to bottom by the Germans who occupied the city. Therefore, Toto could no longer remain in the suite and they had to come up with a plan. The friend decided to give a dinner in honor of the Gauleiter, the district leader of the province. She seated him directly next to Toto, hoping not to arouse his suspicion; it was a risky and audacious move, but the strategy paid off," recalled Lady Deirdre Curteis. "Toto had dressed up, and her entrance turned heads in the dining room. Her presence was so obvious that nobody would have believed that she was a fugitive on the run. They carried on an animated conversation while the Nazis searched the hotel with a fine-tooth comb."

But a few days later, the Germans found and arrested Miss K. in the streets of Venice. "She was immediately sent to Milan," Elisabeth Eichmann said. "I was able to get news about her from an officer I knew but she was being held in a secret location and nobody could reach her. From there, she was sent to the Ravensbrück concentration camp in Germany."

16

Miss K. arrived at Ravensbrück on October 11, 1944, a few days shy of her thirty-sixth birthday. Every deportee was immediately given a number upon arrival, and Toto's was 77370. Political prisoners had to wear red armbands, and hers bore an N for *Niederländerin*, or Dutch.

Built in 1938, Ravensbrück was the country's largest detention camp for women—132,000 women were deported to Ravensbrück and 90,000 exterminated. The camp was situated fifty miles north of Berlin in an area of marshes and dunes swept by glacial winds. The temperature was so cold that the region was referred to as the "little Siberia of Mecklenburg." Toto was imprisoned there for seven months until the camp was liberated by Allied troops in April 1945.

Like Dachau, Buchenwald, Auschwitz, Mauthausen, Sobibor and Treblinka, Ravensbrück was hell on earth, the very incarnation of barbarism and the representation of absolute and unimaginable cruelty. Toto had survived horrific and sordid conditions in Italy but nothing could have prepared her for what came next. She witnessed the construction of the camp's gas chamber in early 1945 and of the second crematorium during the winter.

For a long time, the "undesirables" had been killed by lethal injection but the "turnover" was so great that the Nazis decided to use machine guns to eliminate the unfortunate women. Finding even this task too "tiring," they unanimously opted for gas chambers. Toto would discover that the ashes from the crematorium were used as agricultural fertilizer and that newborns were killed at birth.

Miss K.'s group of detainees included other members of the Resistance: communists, ordinary prisoners, members of religious sects—such as Jehovah's Witnesses—as well as gypsies and Jews. From the moment Toto arrived, she was assigned excavation work, a dreaded and dreadful task. The *verfügbaren*, as they were called, shoveled sand, unloaded trucks and repaired roads. The slightest weakness or moan would be met with a pummeling from the guards.

Waking up at 4:30 A.M., she had to fight to use the toilet facilities, a frightening undertaking in the crowded camp, before heading to a roll call that lasted three hours, regardless of the weather. In rows of ten, the prisoners had to remain still until they received

London, 1934. Toto was in London to shoot a film but soon gave up cinematic pursuits for the life of a femme fatale. Her espionage activities on behalf of the resistance during World War II resulted in her arrest by the Nazis.

The Koopman family in Java (on horseback, from left to right): Toto, her father Colonel Jan George Koopman, her mother Catharina, and her brother Henry, known as "Ody."

Toto and her mother. Mrs Koopman was half-Javanese with Chinese ancestry and she and her children were considered "green Dutchmen," a derogatory reference to the color of their skin. Far from feeling ashamed, Toto was very proud of her biracial heritage, an attitude that was quite rare for the times.

Toto poses for *Vogue*. Thanks to George Hoyningen-Huene, Toto became first biracial celebrity model. Today, Hoyningen-Huene's iconic photographs of Toto are exhibited in museums, published in monographs and featured on postcards.

Alexis Mdivani–bogus prince but authentic rascal–and his wife, American heiress Barbara Hutton. The saga of the "Marrying Mdivanis" caused quite a stir during the 1920s and 1930s. Beautiful and free-spirited, Toto Koopman was Alexis Mdivani's soul mate and siren. He would always have a special place in her heart. Alexis died in a gruesome car accident in 1935, at age thirty.

Toto Koopman and Douglas Fairbanks on the set of the Alexander Korda film *The Private Life of Don Juan* (1934). This is a rare photo, as all of Toto's scenes were left on the cutting room floor.

Toto Koopman (right) and Tallulah Bankhead attend the London premiere of *The Private Life of Don Juan* in 1934. The two women had a brief and intense romance. "My father warned me about men and booze, but he never said anything about women…" Bankhead would respond when asked about her bisexuality.

Toto Koopman in *Vogue*. Wearing creations by Madeleine Vionnet and Augustabernard, Toto Koopman embodied the aspirations of a new generation of women. The gowns clung to the body like a second skin, making it impossible to wear undergarments. To avoid indecency, Toto powdered her breasts and pubic area so that the fabric would not cling to those parts of her body.

Randolph Churchill, son of Winston. Years after his affair with Toto, Randolph Churchill was the first to come to her aid when she was released form the Ravensbrück concentration camp.

Lord Beaverbrook, press baron and one of the most powerful men in Great Britain, with his son Max Aitken. Toto Koopman had affairs with both men, which caused a major scandal.

In 1938, Toto Koopman sat for her friend the painter Joseph Oppenheimer, who had escaped Nazi Germany and come to live in London. "If a portrait can accurately capture one's personality, [Oppenheimer] presents Miss Koopman as a beautiful and alluring woman whose expression reveals a slight disdain mixed with curiosity, a proud reserve and an inherent reticence."

Lady Deirdre Curteis
(then Lady Grantley)
met Toto Koopman
in 1959. The English
aristocrat was young
enough to be her
daughter, and the
two shared a deep
friendship until
Toto's death.

A portrait of Toto Koopman drawn by a
fellow prisoner in Ravensbrück concentration
camp, 1944. There is no trace of the splendid
and proud woman who posed for Joseph
Oppenheimer one year before the war. Toto
would keep this piece of cardboard for the
rest of her life.

Toto Koopman (left) and Elisabeth Eichmann.
The two women met in Italy during the war
and attended a Fascist rally where they both
posed as sympathizers. "The Black Shirts had
no idea that [Toto] was taking mental notes
in order to write up a report for the Italian
Resistance and the British Government,"
Eichmann recalled.

Toto Koopman (left) and Gala Barbisan on the Lido beach, in Venice, summer 1954. Co-founder of the Prix Médicis, Barbisan, a "White Russian," attracted writers to her salons in France and Italy.

Private Collection

Robert Heber-Percy, known as the "Mad Boy." He could be wildly generous or mercilessly cruel, and his violent mood swings justified his nickname. He enjoyed Toto's friendship (a great deal), and the feeling was mutual.

Toto Koopman on an archaeological dig in the Taurus Mountains in Turkey, summer 1953.

Private Collection

Toto Koopman (left) and Erica Brausen, photographed by their friend Willy Maywald at their home in Panarea, summer 1967.

Erica Brausen at the Hanover Gallery. "It was a place where the creative spirit was always alive and where one could see the most brilliant artwork of the time," said Peter Brook.

Francis Bacon. Erica Brausen discovered Bacon in 1946, when he could not sell any of his paintings and no gallery wanted to show his work. She took the risk of representing him and promoted his career. But he would eventually betray her and leave her gallery.

the signal to go to work. Each exhausting workday was followed by an interminable wait for their daily food rations. Toto was worn to the bone. In the fall of 1944, prisoners were allotted two hundred grams (about seven ounces) of moldy bread and a cup of soup each day; it was not unusual to find pieces of rags and dirty bandages floating in the putrid broth. Sleep was nearly impossible. Two to four women shared a thirty-inch mattress, and many simply collapsed from exhaustion to the excrement-covered floor, still wearing their sweat-soaked clothes.

The foul smell was unbearable; vermin infested bodies and epidemics were the prisoners' worst enemies. As one survivor described it: "In the bunks, the sick ones relieved themselves in their beds, too bad for their bunkmates below; the bedding was never washed and we lived with absolute stench, without any hygiene, without any care."[11] The prisoners were on alert even as they slept. "At night, we slept on our shoes that were often filled with snow . . . and with our bread. But still, we often woke to find that everything had disappeared and we would show up at the *Appell* with empty stomachs and bare feet, and for that we were beaten."[12]

Sterilizations were performed on dozens of prisoners, including little girls, during the winter of 1944 to 1945. The victims were mostly gypsies, but Toto Koopman always maintained that she had been subjected to the experiments. In a letter to her friend

Elisabeth Eichmann dated August 15, 1946, in which she discussed her hopes of resuming a normal love life one day, she said that, for the time being "it makes no difference to me at all as I am still impotent from the sterilizing projects of the camp."[13] She spoke of this episode over the years with some modesty but without the slightest ambiguity.

From the moment she arrived, walking past the double rows of SS men and women holding back their German shepherds, from the moment her head was shaved, Toto was prepared for the worst, but daily life at Ravensbrück went beyond anything she could have imagined. "I would have rather been shot immediately!" she often told her friends. Endless roll calls at dawn, even in the snow, prisoners in tattered dresses and barefoot inside their galoshes, dysentery from the polluted water, long lines to use the toilet facilities, which consisted of wood planks with twenty holes in them, not to mention the mood swings of the guards who would kick and beat the prisoners without the slightest provocation. The list of abuses was endless.

At first, Toto turned to faith and prayers to get through her days at the camp. This may seem surprising, as it does not conform to her image as a bisexual vamp. However, her nephew, Robbert J.B. Koopman, pointed out that while their family was Protestant, his aunt converted to Catholicism because she could relate more easily to that religion. "Toto also believed that if one managed to stay clean by washing with one glass of water each day, one could maintain one's dignity and self-esteem. If not, it was certain death," recalled Lady Deirdre Curteis.

Toto's friends maintained that she survived thanks to, curiously, the garlic and onions that Randolph Churchill sent her. Prisoners could receive packages addressed to them with their first and last names, numbers, block numbers and the address of the camp: "Ravensbrück, near Fürstenberg, Mecklenburg, Germany." Knowledgeable about nutrition, Toto recognized that onions and garlic had protective health qualities and could help to ward off sickness. They facilitated the dilation of blood vessels, improved circulation and were an excellent intestinal disinfectant. She believed their antiviral and antibacterial properties protected her from severe illness. Toto claimed Randolph's packages saved her life, and she shared their contents with her fellow prisoners. "When the mail did not come, Toto would exchange her bread rations for onions that were available in the kitchens," added Malitte Matta.

Realizing that she could not endure this existence—especially when the temperatures dropped to minus 27°F during the winter of 1944 to 1945—Miss K. decided to take a chance. What did she risk? Death? Death would be a true deliverance compared to life in the camp. Toto knew, for example, that she might, at any given moment, be assigned to the *Scheisskolonne*, the "column of shit," and the thought paralyzed her with fear. Those unfortunate prisoners had to pick up excrement, press it down with their bare feet and spend entire days in the sewage pit. With their bare hands, they had to mix the vile stuff with the still-warm ashes from the crematorium to form balls that, once dry, would be used as fertilizer. If a prisoner had the misfortune to slip in the midst of this filth, the Nazis set their dogs loose to tear the prisoner to pieces.

17

Miss K. decided she would pretend to be a nurse. Although nurses hardly fared any better than the rest of the prisoners, Toto clung to the slightest hope. "Toto truly believed she was going to die, and summoning her courage, she convinced the SS doctor that she had graduated from St. Mary's Hospital in London, knowing perfectly well that this could never be verified," recounted Malitte Matta. "And her strategy worked! Even she was surprised. She spoke German fluently and that must have helped. This episode was a true measure of her *sangfroid*." When she was sent to Block 6, Toto entered a new circle of hell. Block 6 was Ravensbrück's "death quarters," the most horrific part of the camp, crammed with prisoners suffering from typhoid and cholera.

The medical staff was predominantly made up of German soldiers, but a few nurses were recruited from among the prisoners, particularly in the fall of 1944. These nurses needed nerves of steel to work alongside Nazis who burst out laughing at the sight of rats devouring newborns. Others forced women to undergo abortions, then burned the living fetuses in the furnace. Children were drowned in front of their mothers.

When she arrived in Block 6, Toto discovered an army of living skeletons. Like every area of the camp, Block 6 was overcrowded. SS doctors conducted ghastly experiments on these human guinea pigs and then infected their open wounds out of sheer sadism. Toto and the other prisoner-nurses tried in vain to make bandages out of paper, but these would quickly tear from the pressure of the pus. Gangrene and septicemia were rampant.

Miss K. realized that the sickest prisoners were piled by the dozens into trucks and quickly sent to the gas chambers. This process accelerated in December 1944 as the Third Reich was nearing its end. The SS members tried to destroy anything that could further incriminate them in the eyes of the inquiry commissions that would inevitably be sent by international organizations, starting with the Red Cross. Toto met the terrifying Dr. Winkelmann who was in charge of "selections." He had come from Auschwitz to Ravensbrück for the sole purpose of "optimizing" productivity.

"Nurses who took their task to heart played an essential role," one deportee explained years later.[14] "They had to 'organize,' in other words, to steal from the SS, to cheat. They would order soup for a dying patient who was incapable of swallowing and give it instead to a patient who had a chance of surviving. But, to accomplish this, they had to fool the block commanders, often the other nurses, and sometimes even some of the prisoners. Not only did the nurses have to be crafty; they also had to choose which patients to save, and each decision was a crisis of conscience fraught with heartbreak."

Toto did exactly that, showing remarkable bravery. Heroically courageous, risking everything to try to save as many patients as possible, she would jumble, misplace and falsify patients' charts, causing a slowdown in the otherwise efficient infirmary. She gathered the women who were about to be taken to the gas chambers and hid them in the latrine; she lied about the exact numbers of dead prisoners and redistributed food rations to the weakest patients. She would have been shot on the spot had the SS discovered her activities.

"She showed incredible initiative and tremendous compassion," commented Malitte Matta. "Our friend Philippe de Rothschild learned, later on, that his first wife had died in Toto's arms. Toto had been especially kind to her and he never forgot it." As she emptied the pails of excrement and urine, as she washed and fed the weakest prisoners, Toto tried to cheer them up and lighten the mood.

Even so close to death, the women liked to talk about food and fashion. Toto suddenly had the idea of putting on a fashion show for those in her care. Recapturing the swagger of great Parisian models, she demonstrated to her entranced audience the different ways to wear the striped dress that was the regulation uniform. This very *Koopmanesque* scene was not surprising; Miss K. always knew how to elevate people's moods, even for a few minutes. Her patients adored her.

By February 1945, the organization of the camps faltered as the once remarkable Nazi efficiency began collapsing. Electricity was intermittent and Toto often had to work in the dark. Food distribution was sporadic and many prisoners literally died of hunger. Bodies were tossed into cellars and were gnawed by rats. The crematoria ran day and night and the stench of burning flesh filled the air.

Finally, on April 2, 1945, after endless negotiations with Surhen, the commandant of Ravensbrück, the International Red Cross was able to take charge of the first group of liberated prisoners. "We only survived because of one of Himmler's crazy ideas—the architect of *Jewish genocide* and *extermination through labor* dreamed of succeeding Hitler with the support of the Americans," explained Germaine Tillion, a member of the French

Resistance also imprisoned in Ravensbrück, in *La Traversée du Mal*.[15] "To this end, he would have to write to Eisenhower through a neutral intermediary and without Hitler's knowledge. This explains why, when Count Bernadotte asked him to hand over the remaining survivors of Ravensbrück, Himmler responded, 'Take them.' Had the commandant called Hitler (who was hiding in a bunker in Berlin), Hitler could have ordered that we all be shot. And he would have obeyed."

Toto was released and relocated to Sweden on April 17, 1945, shortly before the camp was officially liberated on April 23. She took only one memento with her, a small piece of cardboard on which a fellow prisoner had drawn her portrait. The drawing—which she kept her entire life before giving it to her nephew, Robbert J.B. Koopman—is haunting. It reveals the face of someone who has seen the heart of evil. There is no trace of the proud and beautiful woman who had posed for Joseph Oppenheimer one year before the war.

There remains one disconcerting story regarding her release. Many close friends assert that Raoul Wallenberg, a World War II hero and one of Israel's Righteous Among the Nations, interceded on Toto's behalf and arranged for her to be released from the camp a few days before the other prisoners. This subject was mentioned in her obituaries in the British press.[16] Wallenberg, a young Swedish diplomat, was an envoy in Budapest. Between July and December 1944, he saved nearly 30,000 Hungarian Jews by providing them with special passports that placed them under the protection of his native country. A deeper investigation has not revealed any connection between Miss K. and Wallenberg. Perhaps the story was sparked by the fact that Toto had personally taken care of the last group of Hungarian Jewish women deported from Budapest.

18

Toto was one of hundreds of deportees of different nationalities rescued by the Red Cross. They relocated Toto to Göteborg, Sweden's second largest city. The health authorities quickly ran out of adequate lodging for the many survivors, and Toto was housed in the paleontology gallery of the city's Natural History Museum. Her bed stood next to a dinosaur skeleton and, Lady Deirdre Curteis recalled, "Toto said this place was the genesis of her future career as an archeologist; during her sleepless nights, she wandered from room to room, studying everything around her."

Haunted by recurring nightmares and memories of the hardship she had endured, Toto was distressed to learn that her father had died in 1942 while she was imprisoned in Italy. Her brother was still alive, though, and Miss K. was anxious to see him again. The state of her health was alarming, according to William

Rospigliosi, because "mistreatment and malnutrition had caused pulmonary weakness." In addition, sterilization procedures had been conducted on her under hideous unsanitary conditions and the mutilations had terrible after-effects on the body. Psychologically, Toto was both aggressive and physically and emotionally exhausted, as revealed by her letters to Elisabeth Eichmann. After surviving four years of imprisonment in Italy and in German death camps, Toto had to start a new life in a world that was in ruins.

Throughout the war, Miss K. had steadfastly and without a moment's hesitation fought for what she believed in—but what would she fight for now? "Randolph Churchill came to her rescue when she was completely alone and in a pitiful state. He restored her sense of hope. He provided her with money, clothing and even a wig, because he knew that camp prisoners had had their heads shaved. It was an incredibly sensitive gesture on his part. He thought of everything," remembered Curteis.

"I was lucky that Randolph Churchill came here and as I am an old love of him [sic], he made a terrible fuss over me and took me all over to Stockholm with him for the papers," Toto wrote to Elisabeth Eichmann from Göteborg. Once Toto had obtained "the papers," she would be able to secure a passport and leave Sweden rapidly. With the monetary assistance she received from the Red Cross, she decided to move to Ascona, on the shores of Lake Maggiore in southern Switzerland, a place that had appealed to her since the early 1930s.

Home to Hermann Hesse and Erich Maria Remarque, Ascona was a favorite destination for artists and hedonists alike. Toto believed no other place could meet her currents needs better. She rented a small house from the German-Swiss banker and art collector Baron von der Heydt and spent her days reading, sleeping, taking walks and, when the weather permitted, swimming. She was still receiving a pension from Lord Beaverbrook.

Miss K. learned that Lord Beaverbrook had further distinguished himself in the interim years, becoming Minister of Supply from 1941 to 1942, and Lord Privy Seal from 1943 to 1945. Max Aitken, the wing commander of an elite Royal Air Force squadron, was now a war hero. Little by little, Toto caught up on all the news of her friends, from Nina Mdivani to Hui-Lan Wellington-Koo—whose husband had just been appointed Chinese ambassador to the United States—as well as Elisabeth Eichmann, now a close friend, who had remained in Italy and worked as an interpreter for the British before moving to Austria in early 1948.

Toto's former suitor Valentine Castlerosse, desolate after his many romantic disappointments, had died of a heart attack in 1943, at the age of fifty-one. Her friend Alexander Korda had produced two films that would become classics in the history of cinema—

The Thief of Bagdad in 1940 and *To Be or Not To Be* in 1942. William Rospigliosi escaped the Italian Fascists and was a correspondent for Time-Life International in New York. Bettina Bergery had not fared so well: her husband had been named Ambassador of the Vichy regime in Moscow and Ankara; after the war, he was brought to justice and eventually acquitted, but Bettina would never again be the flamboyant and provocative woman she once was and many shunned her. And from her villa on the outskirts of Rome, Caresse Crosby founded the Citizens of the World, an organization that sought to prevent future worldwide wars.

Like others who had survived deportation, Toto had to rebuild and redefine her life. While her very survival proved she was stronger than most, she now found herself at loose ends. "We are alive, too bad for us," Germaine Tillion famously said—a feeling that all the survivors shared. Toto was physically unrecognizable: she had lost a great deal of weight and her skeletal appearance worried her friends. And while she marveled at having survived the concentration camps, Miss K. had not yet regained her emotional equilibrium. "She embarked on a reckless love life, drifting from the arms of a bogus Italian duchess to those of an American woman banker," revealed F.C. "Then she met Erica Brausen, who rescued her from chaos."

19

Toto met Erica Brausen, a young German woman, in November 1946, when Brausen was vacationing in Ascona. The two women became inseparable, and during their long walks around Lake Maggiore, Brausen discovered the complexities of Miss K.'s personality. Toto had experienced every possible extreme—life and death, happiness and cruelty, light and darkness. Brausen fell in love with her immediately. For Brausen, love implied devotion, and she wanted to take care of Toto, to protect her and keep her safe. Toto had regained some of her strength, but her body and soul were still recuperating. Europe lay in shambles and the beautiful siren of the 1930s was unrecognizable.

Born on January 31, 1908, Erica Brausen was almost thirty-nine when they met. She and Toto were almost exactly the same age, their birthdays separated by just a couple of months, and had equally strong personalities. The daughter of a Düsseldorf banker, Brausen had only gloomy memories of an unhappy childhood. In a photograph taken when she was six years old—she is at a duck hunt and a shotgun rests on her shoulder—the empty expression on her face reveals the extent of her discontent. Violently opposed to the Nazi doctrine, Brausen eventually left her homeland for good and moved to Paris.

With a small monthly allowance from her father, Brausen lived in Montparnasse, near La Closerie des Lilas, and upon arriving in the city she quickly began to explore its artistic milieux. She spoke impeccable French and spent her days in galleries and artists' studios. Her friends included painters Fernand Léger and Georges Braque, antique dealer Yvonne de Bremond d'Ars, writers Michel Leiris and Raymond Queneau and the avant-garde singer Marianne Oswald, a favorite performer of Bertolt Brecht and Kurt Weill.

Brausen was bisexual and had been involved with both Suzy Solidor and Ernö Goldfinger. Solidor gained fame as a driver for the German General Staff during World War I. She drove ambulances on the front lines, exhibiting the kind of courage that would have made her the pride of her ancestor, the legendary privateer Robert Surcouf. An androgynous beauty, she posed for many painters—Francis Picabia, Maurice de Vlaminck and Tamara de Lempicka among others—and became a famous music-hall singer. Goldfinger was a

Hungarian designer and architect who created furniture for films by Marcel L'Herbier as effortlessly as he designed an actual movie theater. Ian Fleming, with whom he played golf, was so amused by his name that he borrowed it: Goldfinger was one of James Bond's deadliest enemies.

"Erica was not as physically beautiful as Toto. She was smaller, stout, heavier and had a rather brusque demeanor. But her classic features, beautiful eyes, sharp intelligence and great generosity appealed, to a somewhat lesser degree, to both sexes," noted F.C.

In 1935, Brausen's close friend Joan Miró took her to the Balearic Islands. Seduced by the atmosphere of Mallorca, she decided to remain on the island. She opened a bar that quickly became a meeting place for painters and writers. "At the same time, she was making a great deal of money exporting crafts made by local artists. Ceramics and basketry sold like hotcakes throughout Europe and the United States. It was a great commercial success," recounted Malitte Matta.

When Franco came to power, Brausen did not sit idle. "With the help of the American navy stationed nearby, she set up a network for the opposition to flee [the country]. Her code name was Miss Beryl," recounted F.C., "and thanks to her, many members of the opposition made their way past the naval blockade imposed by Franco. Indeed, because of Erica's efforts, Michel

Leiris, Raymond Queneau and their wives were able to escape to Marseille on board an American submarine. They never forgot the help they received from Erica."

Eventually Brausen left Spain for Paris, but the outbreak of war forced her to flee once again. By a stroke of luck, she was able to go to Great Britain. She happened to be traveling at the same time as Hindu guru Meher Baba and his followers. Meher Baba had taken a vow of silence and communicated his teachings in writing. When he learned that the young woman of German origin was sure to be turned away by the British immigration authorities, Meher Baba let her know that he would protect her. She would have to remain with his group of devotees at all times and blend in with the disciples. "And she got through, with the help of painter Anita de Caro, who served as an intermediary between the master and the authorities. Soon after her arrival, a marriage of convenience to a young homosexual allowed her to obtain British citizenship," added F.C.

In London, alone and impoverished, Erica Brausen had to contend with the wary attitude many British citizens held toward Germans. She finally secured a position at the Redfern Gallery, where her knowledge and ability impressed her employers. During the years she frequented the Paris art scene, she had developed, all agreed, an infallible eye. By the time she met Toto Koopman, Brausen had decided to leave the Redfern Gallery and open her own gallery. She had just discovered an unknown painter and wanted to promote his work. His name was Francis Bacon.

Erica Brausen could not leave Toto alone in Ascona. She suggested Toto move to London and that they live together. With no ties to the present, no job and no foreseeable income, Toto, defenseless and dejected, agreed to go.

20

Toto returned to an unrecognizable London. Entire neighborhoods had been obliterated by the air raids of the Blitz. Londoners like Erica Brausen, who had lived through years of blackouts and sirens, were relieved but exhausted. Their weariness was further exacerbated by shortages of food and other goods; rationing in England would last until 1954. When the two women celebrated their first Christmas together in 1946, the general mood of the city was bleak.

Since 1943, Erica Brausen had been living at 26 Bolton Studios, on Gilston Road in Chelsea. In the 1930s, this had been a very elegant address where "serviced apartments" offered round-the-clock amenities. But by 1946, the area had suffered a great deal of damage from the bombardments. The neighborhood may have lost some of its former glamour, but for Toto, it was paradise: there was a small garden, a full-floor studio that served as a living room on the main floor and a foliage-covered skylight. Two bedrooms and a bath comprised the second floor.

Toto needed to regain her stability and Erica lovingly tended to her recovery. Toto saw old friends, strolled through the streets of the city, read and slept—essential steps toward physical and emotional recuperation. Erica bought Toto new clothes—she knew how important the concept of elegance was to her lover. Her budget was limited, so Erica turned to Elspeth Champcommunal, a friend and designer who was the artistic director at the House of Worth in London.

Despite rationing, British designers continued to present their collections and while Erica could not afford the dresses in those collections, she could buy the samples worn by models during the fashion shows. Erica was more masculine than Toto, but her sartorial austerity was also quite stylish. Her only vanity was a bronze Chimera charm bracelet, originally designed by Alberto Giacometti for Elsa Schiaparelli, that she always wore on her right wrist.

Every morning, Toto ate breakfast under the glass skylight and read the day's political news. Miss K.'s friends remember her keen ability to grasp, analyze and predict the consequences of certain political decisions. Indeed, she anticipated the difficulties to come when Great Britain granted independence to India and Pakistan in 1947. Similarly, she expressed deep concerns when the state of Israel was established a year later.

Erica Brausen's solicitude worked miracles and Toto made a spectacular recovery. "When Erica fell madly in love with her, Toto was empty in every sense of the word, but she would soon discover the meaning of true, unconditional love. It was something she had never experienced, as no one had ever treated her this way, not even Max Aitken. Erica was truly smitten with Toto, enthralled by her beauty, her intelligence and her bravery. Love was indeed the best medicine," remembered F.C. "While Toto was not in love with Erica, she did regard her with affection, gratitude and admiration. Coming from Toto Koopman, that was already significant."

Erica realized soon enough that wherever Toto went, she immediately created what could only be described as a gravitational pull. Erica, who was the epitome of discretion, would learn to live with this phenomenon. Stories about Toto's courageous actions during the war began circulating around London, and that might explain the implausible rumor that she had been admitted to White's, London's oldest and most exclusive men's club; perhaps the rumor began because her close friends Stewart Menzies and Randolph Churchill were members of the club. On Churchill's arm, Toto appeared at the Covent Garden Royal Opera House when it reopened in 1946, her first visit since 1939.

Also for the first time in a long time, Toto went to the movies. She saw *The Red Shoes*, whose main character, the tyrannical Pygmalion-like Boris Lermontov, was not inspired by Sergei Diaghilev of the Ballets Russes, as many thought, but by Toto's old friend Alexander Korda. Max Aitken was also making headlines; after serving as a member of Parliament, he had joined his family's newspaper business and was now one of the most influential men of his time. Toto followed his achievements through the press at first, but the former lovers would soon reunite.

Thanks to Erica's generous and benevolent nature, Toto finally emerged from the cloud of darkness that had engulfed her since her release from Ravensbrück. "It is difficult to find it in ourselves, and impossible to find elsewhere," said French writer Nicolas Chamfort about happiness. Yet Miss K. recaptured her *joie de vivre* and serenity through Brausen, who had pulled her from the abyss and helped her leave her difficult past behind.

Even in her darkest days, the notions of self-pity and victimization were foreign to Toto. "Toto returned from the concentration camps without the slightest feeling of hatred, without the slightest feeling of bitterness. She never complained, it was truly startling. So many [survivors] had a desire for vengeance, which was understandable, but not [Toto]," recalled Elisabeth

Eichmann. "I believe that attitude allowed her to regain a more or less normal life."

Finally, Erica involved Toto in her newest project, the creation of her own gallery. Two months before leaving for Ascona, Erica had met a young painter whose work overwhelmed her. Francis Bacon was then completely unknown, and when Erica entered his studio, she stopped short at the sight of his *Painting* (1946): the sides of raw meat and the umbrella in a cage depicted on the canvas struck her as a radically new point of departure for contemporary art.

In his biography of Francis Bacon, British art historian Michael Peppiatt described the painting as "this powerful icon of the mid-twentieth century—which in many ways stands to post-war Europe as *Guernica* did to a world on the eve of self-destruction."[17] Erica bought the painting on the spot. Her main focus from that moment on was to promote Bacon, who had been turned away by all other dealers. The task at hand was considerable, and Toto supported Erica through every step of the process. They had to find financiers and the right location for the gallery Erica envisioned. At that moment, Toto and Erica were as much a business partnership as they were a couple.

21

On May 14, 2008, in New York, a Francis Bacon triptych was sold to a collector for 86.3 million dollars, the highest price ever paid for a work of contemporary art. But sixty-two years earlier, in 1946, Francis Bacon was unable to sell any of his paintings and no gallery would show his work. Only Erica Brausen took the risk of supporting him and launching his career. Through Herculean efforts, she convinced Arthur Jeffress, a rich and eccentric American, to provide the financing.

Jeffress could have stepped out of the pages of a novel by Baron Corvo or Ronald Firbank. An unconventional character, Jeffress divided his time between London and Venice. In the latter city, his extravagance appalled many of the city's older aristocrats, who considered Jeffress an ostentatious and *nouveau riche* homosexual. One of his rumored indulgences was a tool shed designed with mannerist architectural details.

Toto and Erica witnessed his lifestyle first-hand when they visited him in Venice the following summer. He owned a private gondola piloted by handsome young men dressed in white and yellow uniforms that Jeffress had designed himself. Each morning, Jeffress and his guests boarded the gondola and headed to the Lido beaches, where the same gondoliers served an elaborate lunch.

Jeffress agreed to provide Erica the funds to open her gallery and for the time being would be her savior. Erica quickly found the ideal location for her gallery at 32a St. George Street in Mayfair. The space had been used as a fashion showroom in the 19th century and offered wonderful light and excellent proportions. Bacon, usually difficult to please, had only praise for the open space, where subtle daylight showed off his paintings to their best advantage.

Erica chose to name it the Hanover Gallery because of its proximity to Hanover Square. The space was not very large, but it perfectly suited her needs and even had a basement where she could store works in reserve. She selected a red carpet that created a warm atmosphere and placed several fine pieces of Biedermeier furniture around the room. An elegant Louis XV desk sat at the entrance, and it was from behind this desk that Toto and Erica took turns greeting the gallery's visitors.

The Hanover was more than just an art gallery. It immediately became a place to meet and exchange ideas, a destination for conversation and staying *au courant*. Erica and Toto received their guests as if in a salon, and all were welcome. "People also came out of curiosity, to get a first-hand look at the unusual lesbian couple about whom so many stories circulated. The Hanover Gallery's story is also the story of two spies-turned-art dealers and that was intriguing, especially in postwar London," pointed out F.C.

Toto attracted most of the attention. After all, she had modeled for Chanel, appeared on the cover of *Vogue* and had been the talk of London during the "Beaverbrook affair" before becoming an intelligence agent for the Resistance and, ultimately, a concentration camp prisoner. Now she was involved in the launch of an art gallery that would quickly become famous for its bold selections. Like a squid hiding behind its cloud of ink, Miss K. ignored the gossip and never spoke of her mysterious past.

"Her life was like a novel and people came to see her in person," recalled Malitte Matta. "She was aware of it but pretended not to notice. I don't think it even bothered her. Toto never really cared about how others saw her and all her friends knew that about her. She had extraordinary resilience. I have rarely seen anything quite like it."

Since Francis Bacon had not yet produced enough work for a show, Erica decided to feature the artist Graham Sutherland for the gallery's opening show in

June of 1947. Graham Sutherland, along with Henry Moore and a select group of other artists, had been an official artist of the British government during World War II. Sutherland's paintings and drawings illustrating London's devastation from the bombardments and the suffering of the British people as they sought refuge in air raid shelters and survived amidst the rubble were greatly admired.

Sutherland's prestige would increase further with his portraiture of famous men, from Somerset Maugham to Winston Churchill. Although he may have fallen into obscurity today, in 1947 he was one of the country's most renowned artists. The mere mention of his name attracted the public, and so the Hanover Gallery was successfully launched.

Choosing an established painter was a strategic move. Had Erica launched the gallery with a Francis Bacon exhibition, the Hanover might have shut its doors in record time; it was more prudent to establish her reputation as a gallery director before taking a chance with a more shocking exhibition.

Her decision was not based on timidity, but rather on plain good sense. To make her mark on the British art scene, a woman would have to proceed carefully; the slightest misstep in what had been a man's world could prove fatal. Moreover, Erica's German background and her faint guttural accent did not serve her well during the postwar years. Additionally, she openly displayed her love for Miss K. at a time when homosexuality was still a crime punishable by imprisonment in Great Britain, and many disapproved of her lifestyle. Given all the impediments, Erica's success was all the more remarkable.

Toto did her best to support Erica as they worked side by side from morning to night. Their responsibilities were clearly delineated: Brausen dealt directly with artists and selected the works for the gallery, while Totina, as Erica affectionately called Toto, oversaw administrative affairs and planned the gallery's openings, addressing each invitation by hand.

"Between June 1947 and March 1973, the Hanover Gallery sent out over two million invitations to the 309 exhibitions organized by Erica," recalled F.C. "Using the correct form of address was often a complex task in Great Britain; Toto excelled at matters of etiquette in all its nuances. She would never confuse 'Honorable' with 'Right Honorable' or 'Sir' with 'Lord.' They worked in this manner through the late 1960s before deciding to simplify things."

In the years leading up to the war, Miss K. knew everyone in London and she now invited all the important people to the gallery. "Erica was proud and loved to say that the Hanover owed its success to Toto's address book," recalled F.C. Malitte Matta agreed, saying, "My husband and I understood immediately that it was both important and useful for Erica to have a woman like

Toto by her side. She had the *savoir-vivre* and *savoir-faire* to mingle easily with the rich and famous potential buyers. Erica was more practical and harder to approach; she concentrated on the artists, while the spectacularly beautiful and elegant Toto hosted the *vernissages,* introducing painters and sculptors to various art collectors with perfect charm and natural ease. Their collaboration worked perfectly; it was very smooth." In short, Erica recognized that artistic success could not be achieved without the right social contacts.

Toto began each day by updating the gallery's files—changes of address, marriages, deaths. Nothing escaped her vigilance. Each morning she carefully scanned the obituaries published in the *Times* and the *Daily Telegraph* to keep her files current. She also supervised the mailing of catalogues and filed articles in the press book.

After the Graham Sutherland exhibition, Erica showed the work of several unremarkable artists as she waited for Francis Bacon to complete enough paintings for a show. His one-man exhibition was held at the Hanover Gallery from November 8 to December 10, 1949 and marks an important event in the history of art. "I remember the *vernissage* perfectly," said Gianna Sistu. "I was a young girl at the time and had attended the opening with my mother. Londoners were shocked—they had never seen such violence—and some of them were visibly shaken and livid. Bacon watched, thrilled, while Toto and Erica moved from group to group as if nothing unusual was happening. The contrast was rather comical. But the fact remains that Bacon revolutionized the way people saw [art] and he owed it all to Erica."

22

When Erica Brausen met Francis Bacon—Graham Sutherland introduced them during the summer of 1946—she was instantly stunned by his work and its mix of horror and exceptionally vibrant energy. Erica paid 350 pounds for his *Painting* (1946), a considerable sum at the time, especially for a work by an unknown artist. She did not bargain then, nor would she ever; she simply agreed to pay his asking price. Bacon, who was mistrusting by nature, found a kindred spirit in Erica. From that moment on, they would meet regularly to exchange ideas at the Ritz bar or in his Cromwell Place studio.

Brausen was fascinated by this rebellious man, whose sharp and poisonous personality, precisely etched in every aspect of its dissonance, seemed inseparable from his work: one explained the other. By this time, Bacon was shaping his own reputation with the greatest care, and it was he who started the rumors that circulated about him. According to Francis Bacon, his violent father, a horseman, had his son horsewhipped by the grooms to whom Francis would later grant sexual favors—forever linking sexuality and sadomasochism in his mind. The relationship between father and son turned even more venomous when the elder Bacon discovered his son trying on his mother's underwear and banished him from home. That moment would mark the start of the Baconian odyssey.

In London, Bacon lived in hotels, leaving without paying the bill and turning to petty theft when the need arose. He made his way to Berlin, a city whose decadence suited him perfectly, and then to Paris, where his dandy-ruffian personality became even more sharply defined. He discovered the works of Picasso and visited the slaughterhouses—the memory of those meat carcasses would haunt his work for years. And quite by chance, he attended the birthday party of a famous model—Toto Koopman. She took no notice of him, but he never forgot that moment.

Back in London, Bacon pursued his bad boy lifestyle. Living on the fringes suited him, and he reveled in behaving provocatively. He began to paint and participated in several group shows but his work, including his first *Crucifixion* (1933) went unnoticed. He was leading a colorful existence: he lived with his former governess and his lover. The penniless and improbable threesome moved regularly and, as they rarely had enough beds, Nanny Lightfoot often slept on the kitchen table. To make ends meet, Bacon, who could be quite seductive, never hesitated to offer his services as a gigolo. Before meeting a client, he would brush his teeth with scouring powder, slick his hair with black shoe polish and apply outrageous makeup, then slip on fishnet stockings under his trousers.

Bacon could not sell his paintings and survived by setting up clandestine gambling sites. He spent the war years in London after the army discharged him due to the severe asthma attacks that had plagued him throughout his life. Bacon met Erica at the very moment he was about to give up on a painting career.

Brausen was nobody's fool and understood immediately that Bacon's histrionics were a facade. The artist shielded himself from everything, including his memories, by hiding behind his outrageous behavior. During their long conversations, Brausen learned that his childhood, spent on a stud farm in Ireland, had left him with wounds that would never heal; traces of those wounds can be found in his paintings. His typically British family was living in Ireland when the country was under British domination and Sinn Féin and the IRA were trying to rid the country of the occupiers. Like other British citizens who lived nearby, young Francis was permanently on alert and felt as if he were being followed, a theme that would always be present in his work. Erica was moved by his story and grew convinced she could help him just as she had Toto, albeit for different reasons. Within the space of three months, Erica had met the two most important people in her life.

But when Erica introduced Bacon to Toto, he disliked her immediately. The relationship between Bacon and Erica was intense and the jealousy he felt toward Erica's lover and muse was irrevocable. "In her presence, he would be charming, but behind her back, Bacon called her 'the Javanese whore.' His behavior toward her was truly hateful, because he knew that she came first in Erica's heart; [Toto] had dethroned him in the space of three months," recalled F.C.

Still, the painter had to learn to deal with Toto. His paintings did not sell easily, but Erica had agreed to cover his substantial financial needs. Bacon was a gambler and often lost large sums of money in casinos. He regularly left London for Monte Carlo or Cannes and would harass Erica by mail from a distance. Bacon kept pressing her to send him more money and the situation became increasingly difficult: funds leaving the country were closely monitored in the postwar years, and only a small amount of cash could be taken out at a time.

Erica relied on Toto to bring Bacon large sums of cash. It was a risky proposition: if Toto were caught at the frontier, she would face costly fines and even prison time for a second offense. But Toto was unfazed and saw it as a way to express her gratitude for all Erica had done for her. Bacon was therefore obliged to thank the woman he considered his enemy.

Well aware of his spiteful feelings, Miss K. avoided argument and adopted a condescending and slightly ironic attitude toward the painter. Caught in the middle, Erica did her best to keep things amiable. On opening nights, the threesome posed for photographs, side by side, all smiles—no one could have guessed what was going on behind this carefully staged facade.

Erica faced other difficulties: how to convince her protégé to entrust her with his paintings, especially the ones that didn't please him, which he often destroyed. Erica nevertheless succeeded in holding yearly exhibitions of Bacon's works at the Hanover Gallery from 1949 to 1959—1956 was the only exception. Only today can one fully appreciate the extent of Brausen's efforts to organize these shows within that time frame. Moreover, the paintings were difficult to sell because their subject matter was too disturbing for the times. Years later, Toto could still recall the looks of horror worn by many visitors when they saw the paintings of screaming popes and decomposing animal carcasses. Seated at her desk at the front of the gallery, she tried, as best she could, to keep a straight face.

Brausen's relentless efforts to promote Bacon's work eventually paid off; she knew she had reached a turning point when she sold *Painting* (1946), the first of his works to have caught her attention, to the Museum of Modern Art in New York in 1948. She established a small group of collectors who began, albeit timidly, to collect Bacon's paintings; Robert and Lisa Sainsbury were among them. Brausen had propelled Bacon's works to the forefront, "ensuring that the pictures were brought to the attention of the most influential members of the art world not only in Britain, but in Europe and in America."[18]

23

Following forays into the worlds of fashion, film, jour-
nalism and political diplomacy, Toto turned to the
European art scene. From 1947 to 1973, Toto often
accompanied Erica on her visits to artists' studios as
they searched for promising new talent. They attended
many openings to see what other gallery owners were
showing, and Toto and Erica were photographed at all
the major international art events, such as the Venice
Biennale. The rivalry between galleries was fierce, and
Erica knew it was crucial to find new ideas and contin-
uously surprise and astonish the collectors who closely
watched her work.

Adding to this constant pressure was the fact that
Arthur Jeffress, the gallery's financial benefactor,
detested Francis Bacon's paintings. Jeffress suddenly
decided to back out as an investor because he could no
longer fathom the idea of supporting the painter. Erica

found herself on tenterhooks at the very moment the Hanover Gallery was taking off, as she no longer had the funds to pursue her work.

Bankruptcy was looming when one night a man walked into the empty gallery. Michael Behrens was a banker who was immediately fascinated by Bacon's work. When he learned of Brausen's financial difficulties, he offered to help. "The next day, he was the new owner of a place whose existence he knew nothing about the day before," recalled F.C. "The paintings stayed on the walls and the Hanover Gallery remained open. Behrens had great admiration for Erica, even if he was sometimes at a loss to express it. He was a banker after all."

The couple's close friends often wondered how Erica managed to deal with the constant worry and pressure. Her secret was G.I. Gurdjieff. To some Gurdjieff was a great spiritual leader, but to others he was an accomplished thief. Erica aligned herself with the first group.

A legendary figure of esoteric philosophy, George Ivanovich Gurdjieff was and still is a source of both controversy and admiration. A discussion of Gurdjieff and his philosophy's multiple ramifications requires not only a keen mind but also a calm, cautious and tactful approach. His principles were based on the integration of all vital energies, with the idea of finding harmony between them as well as with the cosmic order. His doctrine is complex and must be studied with the utmost rigor or it remains puzzling.

Gurdjieff's biography was equally intriguing and disconcerting: even those closest to him offered contradictory views of his personality. One could not have invented such a life. His was the story of a half-Greek, half-Armenian boy born around 1866 to a poor family from the Caucasus, who left his impoverished homeland as an adolescent to discover the world. Curious and impatient, and gifted with what were then called "psychic powers," he traveled throughout Central Asia with the help of secret Armenian societies.

Gurdjieff presented himself as a professional healer. Using his power of persuasion and his knowledge of hypnosis, he cured many alcoholics in the small towns he visited. He traveled on to Tibet, India, Mongolia, Ethiopia and Egypt, through the Gobi desert and as far as the Solomon Islands. He acquired vast and varied knowledge during his years of travel, and this knowledge would be the basis for his future theories.

For nearly three decades, Gurdjieff associated with dervishes and lamas, read the works of Plato and the teachings of Rosicrucianism, studied cosmology and theosophy as well as Assyrian and Sufi texts. He assembled a group of disciples, recruited from mysterious circles, and founded the Institute for the Harmonious Development of Man.

The methods he advocated—wherein ideas borrowed from different cultures were combined with his specific vision, having nothing to do with any past, recognized or secret tradition—were not intended for hermits who sought silence and meditation. On the contrary, his methods were meant to help his contemporaries experience full lives in relation to family, work, love and sexuality. Therein lies the modern aspect of his research: he believed in an intimate connection between one's inner and public lives. He illustrated these beliefs with a nine-pointed geometric figure that he called an "enneagram." This diagram shows the nine essential points needed to weaken the conditioning to which all people have been subjected since childhood and point the way toward a life free of passivity and illusory choices.

Gurdjieff was brutal and showed no mercy toward those who wanted to learn how to create energy that was free of the destructive forces linked to our time on earth. While it might seem paradoxical, he truly believed he was helping others by humiliating them in thousands of different ways. In his view, one could only attain elevated spirituality by rejecting praise and admiration. Reaching a higher level of consciousness demanded constant courage and adaptability.

His very specific teachings were based on group work and precise and varied exercises that included sacred dances, the participation of mediums and the practice of different forms of breathing intended to coordinate the mind and the body. Some of his disciples, who abandoned everything to follow him, could not understand why they had to perform difficult domestic tasks or why they were awakened in the middle of the night to leave their warm beds and go sleep in cold and damp rooms. Gurdjieff would even shame them in front of the other participants or demand that they publicly confess their failings in great detail.

Some of his initiatives were scandalous, and his critics were quick to mention the case of Katherine Mansfield, the writer suffering from tuberculosis who took refuge at his side in 1922. At the time, Gurdjieff and his followers lived in France, near Fontainebleau; he advised Mansfield, who had become a shadow of herself, to sleep in the barn, under the pretext that the emanations of ammonia from the cows' breath would cure her disease. Instead, the cold conditions and bizarre therapy precipitated her death in record time. For all these reasons, Erica's commitment to Gurdjieff was not widely supported by her friends. "I have a very negative view of Gurdjieff. I found him appalling," revealed Edmonde Charles-Roux. And Raoul Tubiana, a renowned French hand surgeon and longtime friend of Toto and Erica, was quick to add, "I thought he was a Rasputin-like guru, and as a scientist I could not understand the appeal of his theories."

Brausen met Gurdjieff in Paris in the early 1930s. His work groups had caught the attention of intrigued followers, and Erica was especially interested in The Rope, a group exclusively for women taught jointly by Gurdjieff and Jane Heap, an American disciple. Jane Heap was editor-in-chief of *The Little Review*, a literary magazine known for its high standards that ceased publication in 1929, after Heap had begun to follow Gurdjieff. When Gurdjieff asked Heap to move to London in 1935 to expand the reach of his teachings, she quickly agreed. She arrived in London at the start of World War II, and Erica joined her group soon after.

"Jane had enormous wealth of knowledge and humanity. She was very straightforward, very level-headed with a marvelous sense of humor," recalled Peter Brook who, with his wife, actress Natasha Parry, worked alongside her. "We met every week at her Hamilton Terrace home. Members shared their thoughts. There was nothing didactic about it; we all contributed our own experience and impressions. Jane motivated us and would not hesitate to mock us the way Gurdjieff would. She proposed exercises that involved sacred dervish dances, breathing and coordination. Some of the movements were very difficult, and you had to be sufficiently open so that each part of the body could function independently while you moved in ways that were completely contradictory. Your hands moved to one rhythm, your feet to another and your head to yet another. It was not a question of ability but of inner harmony. Sometimes we acted out a play or prepared a meal to be shared together. Jane was very down-to-earth and we had to live in the moment, be committed and connected to reality. Gurdjieff's doctrine was not abstractly esoteric."

Jane Heap devised an exercise that reflected those priorities. In order to be useful and express their appreciation for well-executed manual work, each member of the group was required to find an old broken toy at a flea market or an antiques dealer, buy the toy at a reasonable price and restore it with the greatest care and attention. The toys were then resold at The Rocking Horse, the shop in the Swiss Cottage neighborhood of London owned by Jane and her partner, stylist Elspeth Champcommunal.

"Erica was a wonderful friend," added Peter Brook, "and when we met, she was still working at the Redfern Gallery. For many years, my wife and I were close with her, but not intimately close, because she was rather discreet and secretive. We were mainly work friends, but we did share many happy meals. We attended openings at the Hanover, and Erica came to the premieres of my plays with Toto, who was warm, vivacious and intelligent."

Miss K. was quite fond of Peter Brook and Natasha Parry and followed their work closely. Toto's friends remember that she admired Brook's talent and spoke of his work as a director with contagious enthusiasm. In the following years, Brook and Parry were always welcomed on Panarea, the Aeolian island where Toto and Erica would spend their later years.

It is unknown whether Toto ever met Gurdjieff herself, but Erica is known to have visited him regularly in Paris until his death on October 29, 1949. Toto had also joined Jane Heap's work group, and through it she discovered a level of discipline and a degree of understanding that she had never known before. She recognized that different facets of life could gravitate naturally around an interior axis as long as one remained vigilant and focused. The complicity of the initiated and the shared taste for esoteric subjects further strengthened the bond between Toto and Erica.

24

The Hanover Gallery presented its first exhibition of Francis Bacon's work in 1949, a year that marked an important moment in the history of 20th-century art. For Toto, it also represented a time of great personal loss. Her brother, Ody, suffered a fatal heart attack in Holland at the age of forty-seven. She had been so happy to reconnect with him and resume their relationship after the war. And now he was gone. Always sensitive to her companion's slightest mood changes, Erica realized that Toto was still vulnerable and watched over her even more closely.

Publicly, Toto fought to remain in perfect control but Erica knew her too well to be fooled. Toto's calm appearance was an illusion; at the first sign of trouble, she shut down emotionally. Four years after her release from the concentration camps, Toto had lost her only link to the past, to the Javanese childhood of which she spoke with so much tenderness, and she was shaken. It seemed she would never be free of sorrow.

Erica knew that Toto did not derive real satisfaction from the work she did at the gallery. During this period of grief and mourning, she encouraged Toto to follow her own interests and not dwell in sadness. When Miss K. revealed that she dreamed of becoming an archaeologist, Erica immediately financed her studies. "For Toto, Erica was a marvelous umbrella that shielded and protected her from everything. For Erica, Toto was a guardian angel who always encouraged her to do her best, to continually surpass herself; the Hanover Gallery would never have succeeded as it did if Toto were not at Erica's side," said F.C.

Toto enrolled as an independent student at the Institute of Archaeology at the University of London. After a lifetime of rebelling against rules and strict regulations, Toto was an exemplary student. She still spent part of her mornings at the Hanover Gallery with Erica, but all her afternoons were dedicated to her studies. She worked hard, did research for her presentations at the British Museum and at the libraries of Oxford University, attended numerous conferences and even took a photography course so that she could document all the artifacts uncovered during a dig. Her readings included many scientific reports and were a testimony to the commitment and seriousness she brought to her studies.

With Erica's support, Toto was able to channel her sadness into a source of inspiration. Within a short time, she was working in the field and participating in archaeological excavations—combining practice and theory—and her morale improved quickly. Erica, who had always believed in Toto's abilities, was filled with pride when Toto received her diploma. From that moment on, Toto always listed her profession as archaeologist when she filled out her passport forms.

Seton Lloyd and Max Mallowan, two internationally known archaeologists, were Toto's mentors during the 1950s. Like Toto, Seton Lloyd had taken an indirect path to archaeology. He supported Toto at each stage of her studies and even offered her the chance to work alongside him on an excavation in Turkey, which she happily accepted. Max Mallowan was a specialist in ancient Middle Eastern history, and Toto worshiped him. The charismatic Mallowan had been teaching at the University of London since 1947, and Toto would not have missed his lectures for anything in the world. She participated in several excavations in Iraq with Mallowan who, incidentally, was married to Agatha Christie.

Toto prepared for her trips with the utmost care, never overlooking a single detail. She studied Turkish for several years so that she could function independently once she was on site. While not completely fluent, she quickly became proficient, a talent that was not surprising for a woman who already spoke Dutch, English, French, German and Italian.

During the war, Miss K. had survived by developing manual dexterity and her abilities would prove very useful during her trips throughout the Middle East. When she arrived at a camp, after several days of travel in trucks filled with equipment and supplies, Toto was handed sheets and towels and, in certain places, an *aftabeh*, a watering container used in lieu of toilet paper. Water was brought in on the backs of donkeys and was rationed, making washing up a quick affair at best. There was danger everywhere and the archaeologists had to contend with scorpions, snakes, swarms of mosquitoes, lice or streams of mud, depending on the season. In such remote areas, even a rabid dog's bite could be deadly.

Each morning, dressed in a simple shirt, linen pants and a big straw hat, Toto set to work. She scratched, brushed, dusted, restored, classified and photographed with total concentration. Focusing intensely on the work at hand was her way of forgetting the past. The world of archaeology was a place where she could renew herself, both physically and spiritually. None of Toto's colleagues knew who she was, and she enjoyed the anonymity. She would reveal her identity only under duress or specific circumstances, as she did during a dig in Jordan in 1956.

When, during that expedition, the local authorities restricted the team's access to certain sites, Toto was able to convince the representative of the British government and the Hashemite sovereign himself to let them move about freely. Toto's contacts were a precious resource in the situation, and she did not hesitate to revert to the methods of a privileged woman and employed them. Over the next ten years, she participated in excavations, usually twice each year; she blended in with the groups and was happy to be inconspicuous. She also attended meetings organized by the British School at Athens that promoted the study of Greek archaeology.

Toto was always eager to speak about her trips—to Lebanon, Egypt and Iraq—in her letters or in conversation with her friends, and none of them would forget her delightful recounting of a trip to Turkey during the summer of 1953. She had left Ankara on her own and headed south to meet up with an archaeological team in the Taurus Mountains.

On this particular day, Toto started out early to avoid the midday heat of the Anatolian plains. She boarded a bus filled with local farmers whose clothes looked as if they were held together with pieces of multicolored fabric. This had nothing to do with hardship; in fact, these people were rather well off. Those pieces of material sewn here and there were actually the latest fashion trend, a random aesthetic expression of style.

Toto's fellow travelers brought their own food—mainly bread, onions and cucumbers—and the conviviality was such that she felt as if she had been invited to a friendly and festive picnic. Her fellow travelers were intrigued by her presence. Lest they wonder about her marital status, she invented a husband and children whose number varied over the course of her travels. She had not yet mastered Turkish, and her hesitation when she tried to express herself was as amusing to the people she met as her colorful family stories. At one point, everyone settled down to listen to a young boy sing wistful tunes accompanied by a small terracotta drum.

They finally left the scorching Anatolian plains for the Taurus Mountains with their green slopes covered with flowers, pine trees and cypress trees. The bus slowed down as it approached the narrow precipices. The streams, fed by melting snow, provided welcome relief from the heat. Toto liked to imagine that she was following the road taken by Alexander the Great, and inscriptions in Greek on a nearby rock seemed to confirm this.

They arrived without incident in Adana, the area's prosperous albeit unattractive capital. Miss K. spent only one night there but made a point of visiting the mosque, where she viewed the city's archaeological treasures. She had to leave the next morning to reach Karatepe, situated on an isolated hilltop, where

Toto would meet Halet Çambel from the University of Istanbul. Çambel and her colleague, Helmuth Bossert, had discovered a Hittite site from the 7th century B.C.E., a fortified citadel with two doorways guarded by statues of lions and sphinxes.

Toto left Adana in a dilapidated bus. The driver had decorated the inside of the vehicle with his own paintings, which were attached to each other with ribbons and knots of dyed fabric. He offered her the seat next to his, near a pink plastic parrot set on springs, and Toto accepted the place of honor. The road was full of potholes and the journey was bumpy, but Toto nevertheless enjoyed the ride that took her past the ruins of castles that dated back to the Crusades.

Many hours later, she arrived in the village of Kadirli. From there, she had planned to rent a horse to reach Karatepe, Turkish for "black hill." Coincidentally, however, the Jeep carrying the month's supplies was leaving Kadirli for Karatepe at the same time, so she could ride by vehicle instead. The man at the wheel drove at full speed; that she arrived in one piece was a miracle. Toto was thrilled to be reunited with Çambel, a woman for whom she had great admiration. She scrutinized every detail of her new surroundings: the scenery, the fauna and flora, the indigenous people, the Hittite citadel—the reason she was on the site—and the daily activities of the excavation team. She would spend three months there, doing her part for the mission.

On her last day, Toto left on horseback at 3:00 A.M. to return to Kadirli; from there, she made her way to Ankara, where Erica was waiting for her. The two women then spent the month of August traveling to Baalbek, Damascus, Beirut, Jerusalem, Bethlehem, Alexandria, Athens and other cities. They visited the Acropolis on September 6, 1953 and, after a detour to Corfu and another to Venice, they returned to London. But their happiness was short-lived, as Erica was about to learn that Francis Bacon had betrayed her. While she was away, he had agreed to show his work in another gallery.

25

Plagued by mounting gambling debts, Francis Bacon took advantage of the Hanover Gallery's annual summer closing, in August 1953, to contact Helen Lessore, founder of the Beaux Arts Gallery on Bruton Place, who immediately agreed to buy several of his paintings. Erica Brausen was devastated by the news and went directly to the gallery to try and buy back the paintings. Lessore refused to sell them and planned a small exhibition of Bacon's works in November 1953. The Hanover Gallery would never close its doors again, even in the summer. "Erica often spoke about Bacon's money problems," said Giannu Sistu. "She advanced him large amounts of money, but it was never enough. What's more, he always struggled to give her enough work in due time. It was exhausting for her."

Bacon's actions were all the more insulting because Brausen had done so much for him. That very year,

1953, she had organized his first New York show at Durlacher Brothers. Moreover, "since Brausen seems to have worked on a slender profit margin... Bacon could already be counted among the very few experimental artists... who made any kind of basic living from their work."[19]

Miss K. recognized the extent of her companion's distress and did all she could to lift her spirits. She showered Erica with generosity, grace and tenderness, taking her to see Herbert von Karajan conduct Sibelius' "Symphony No. 5," inviting friends to dinner—among them, Sonia Orwell, widow of the author of *1984*, Peter Brook and Natasha Parry and Hans Arp, a painter and sculptor whose work had been shown at the Hanover Gallery. Their guests also included the high-spirited Gala Barbisan who had arrived in London in early November. Her presence was a spectacle in itself, for better or worse.

Married to a French industrialist, Gala Barbisan was a White Russian who held salons in her Montmartre home in Paris and in her Cortina d'Ampezzo chalet, as well as in Venice, where invitations to her summertime Lido beach luncheons were highly prized. She was enchanted by Toto's unusual personality and wry humor, and the two women remained close for more than forty years. Gala Barbisan was the co-founder of France's Médicis Prize for literature and spent a great deal of time in the company of writers. She always introduced the latest prizewinners to Toto who, as a result, met Curzio Malaparte, Alain Robbe-Grillet and Jean Genet. "Toto wanted to befriend Jean, but nothing came of it," remembered Edmonde Charles-Roux. "He said he immediately understood where she was headed and he refused to become the bad boy genius she wanted to add to her collection of eccentric people."

Gala Barbisan was a capricious and spoiled woman who behaved abominably when she did not get her way. When Erica Brausen refused to show the work of one of Gala's protégés at the Hanover Gallery, Barbisan planned an act of revenge befitting her eccentricity. She did not raise a fuss or show any signs of anger. Instead, one day, she came to have tea with Toto and Erica; after she left, they discovered a bloodstain on the expensive silk-upholstered gold-leaf Empire chair in which Barbisan had been sitting. Barbisan, who was menstruating, had expressed her displeasure—her friends chose to take it in good humor. Toto had always sought out exiled Russians, and Gala Barbisan was in good company with Hoyningen-Huene, the Mdivanis, Iya Abdy and Moura Budberg.

Erica had seen fads come and go, and by this time, very little could surprise her. The Hanover Gallery showed the work of artists who were famous for their idiosyncrasies. Exhibitions of the work of Max Ernst, Lucian Freud, Meret Oppenheim—whose fur-covered teacup had caused quite a stir—and Marcel Duchamp, transformed the gallery into an ongoing "happening." Erica and Toto always had a penchant for the unusual, but the morbid fascination of certain artists left even these two women perplexed. One day, they were visiting the studio of Lucian Freud, whom they represented, when the artist proudly displayed to them several jars he kept under his bed that contained his girlfriends' aborted fetuses.

On a lighter note, the two women learned that one of their brokers, a former member of the Belgian Resistance, had devised a singular way of transporting Erica's paintings from Paris to England. Believing that the price paid in Paris was already high enough, she wanted to avoid any additional duty charges, so she simply rolled up the canvases and hid them in the folds of her enormous Watteau-style beret—a subterfuge that worked every time.

The Hanover Gallery's reputation for eccentricity had grown, and openings turned into events that people still remember today, forty years after the gallery's closing. Pol Roger champagne flowed freely and large crowds gathered as they would have for a theatrical performance. Erica and Toto never failed to delight both the artists and the guests.

In 1954, when the gallery paid tribute to Russian painter Pavel Tchelitchew, Erica and Toto asked their friend Edith Sitwell to read one of her poems. A rather unattractive woman, the British poet always tried to live up to her own motto, "If one is a greyhound, why try to look like a Pekingese?" She planned her entrances with great care and would not hesitate to arrive on a stretcher in an ambulance if it suited her mood at the time. She dressed flamboyantly, in the style of a Madonna from the Quattrocento, and was always the center of attention. Sitwell remarked that if she were to turn up in ordinary clothes, it would cause people to doubt the existence of God.

Young artist Niki de Saint Phalle, who was still unknown in England, was greeted by an all-woman band that played the American anthem at the opening of her first London show. At the time, she had not yet chosen to become a French national. Toto always found original ways to surprise the artists as well as the guests.

Thanks to Brausen's discerning and intelligent selections, the Hanover Gallery quickly became London's premier avant-garde gallery and the gateway to contemporary art. The Hanover, the Galerie Berggruen in Paris and the Galerie Beyeler in Basel were considered to be Europe's three most outstanding galleries. As the Hanover's success grew, Brausen redecorated the space, replacing the red carpet with Carrara marble. She hired assistants; the team included Tutu Antonius, Michael Greenwood and a young Frenchman.

"I met Toto and Erica in 1953 through a mutual friend," recounted the Frenchman. "We had lunch together, and I was intrigued by this couple about whom there were so many fantastic rumors. I had already heard about Toto's past adventures as a spy and that her grandmother was an Indonesian princess. I remember her so vividly that day. She was distant and forthcoming at the same time. She had impeccable manners and extraordinary composure. She was a keen observer and nothing escaped her attention. She was so sophisticated; she knew people throughout Europe and spoke several languages fluently. She spoke to me in perfect French without the slightest accent and with an extraordinary vocabulary. And it was the same in English, German or Italian. A priceless asset for a spy, it goes without saying. I realized right away that these two women operated by what sailors call 'dead reckoning.' There was no middle ground between respect and intolerance, and they could turn on you in an instant."

The young Frenchman wanted to remain in London and was looking for work. Brausen offered him a job at the Hanover Gallery. At the time, obtaining a work permit was a complex procedure because one had to prove that a British citizen, who would have priority over a foreigner, could not fill the position in question. Brausen explained to the authorities that her gallery showed works by artists from all over the world and that she needed a French secretary to present their work to French collectors. "That was how I started, she used to call me her *tea-boy*. I took care of everything—

framing, hanging, deliveries, correspondence. I even designed a new letterhead for their stationery."

After three years at the gallery, the young man and his boyfriend benefited from Brausen's enormous generosity. "We were living in a friend's apartment but it was a temporary situation. A studio became available on the Boltons, where Erica and Toto lived. Erica took over the lease, had the place repainted at her cost and handed me the key. It was magnificent, with sixteen-foot ceilings, wide windows, wonderful light and it was quiet. It was truly an extraordinary gift. She could be harsh, but also very generous."

Finally, in 1961, Brausen also hired her friend Yvonne Robinson-Knapp to work at the gallery. She recalled, "I met Erica in 1954 when she showed the work of my companion, painter Stefan Knapp. We had dinner together at the Gilston Road apartment and I was immediately enchanted by the personalities of the two women. Toto was elegant, with a touch of eccentricity, and I still remember that she was wearing a ballerina's tutu as an evening dress, which was rather unusual in the 1950s. Erica was more low-key but did have one charming oddity: she wore only one earring, a small blackamoor, one of those African heads encrusted with precious stones. People were always saying to her, 'Oh, you have lost one of your—' 'No, no,' she would answer, laughing . . . It had become a game. They spoke French to each other and were wonderful hostesses. Nobody cooked pheasant and grouse like Erica. They exhibited the same degree of refinement as they did at the Hanover Gallery. For example, Erica disliked 'office furniture,' so we would be typing letters on portable typewriters that rested on inlaid tables; the tables were so highly polished that the typewriters kept sliding as if on a skating rink. It was impossible to be bored in such a place, as fascinating people were always turning up. Who could forget Parisian gallery owner Alexander Iolas with whom Erica worked very closely? He would breeze in wearing a long fur coat that reached the ground, followed by a bevy of harried young people. On Saturday mornings, Toto came to pick up Erica and they would go shopping in Soho's French boutiques. It was a ritual whenever Toto was in London. I realize today that Erica had an extraordinary flair for recognizing talent before anyone else. She was the first gallery owner to organize a Botero retrospective in England and the first to understand that future film director Derek Jarman, one of her protégés, was going to become an important artist. She was never wrong."

26

Throughout the 1950s, Toto and Erica supported and sustained each other, never failing to meet each other's needs. Their friends never witnessed a single fight, disagreement or grievance between them. Balancing their varied interests, they divided their time between the gallery, archaeological pursuits, travel, Gurdjieff's work groups and a full schedule of cultural and social activities. Had Toto really put her vamp years behind her? Not quite.

Toto's strong sexual appetite led her to renew her relationship with Max Aitken. Max, who had married three times, became her lover once again. They met regularly during the week, in the middle of the day, in a bachelor apartment. Miss K. also had an affair with writer and journalist William Rospigliosi, with whom she had been imprisoned in Italy. "Toto always had lovers, even when she was very old. The men were usually famous, married and in positions of power," recalled Malitte Matta. "In the beginning, Erica was amused by it."

Erica was also having an affair, with Rachel S., the attractive wife of a London banker. All of this took place in a very civilized atmosphere. Toto liked Erica's mistress and often invited her to lunch. "There was not a shred of hypocrisy in Toto," said Lady Deirdre Curteis. "She approached life's complexities with a clear head and goodwill, especially when it came to sex."

After Erica and Toto had been together several years, Erica realized she would have to accept Toto's needs—her relationships with men, her wanderlust—or Miss K. would succumb to boredom as others would succumb to an illness. As Toto's happiness was Erica's main concern, she granted Toto complete freedom. Toto was very casual about sex, which she viewed as a very pleasant form of exercise and entertainment. She would never have considered leaving Erica and for the time being, Erica was reassured—but her tolerance of Toto's lifestyle would eventually take its toll. To Toto's credit, in order to spare Erica's feelings, she was always tactful and circumspect about her indiscretions. She was a master juggler.

Erica's insecurities were put to rest when she, along with all their friends, realized that Toto would never leave. Their *modus vivendi* was based on that certainty: Toto lived by her own rules and Erica accepted them.

Miss K. was the only person with whom Erica could, in all confidence, discuss and evaluate business opportunities—a fact that explained certain compromises. Neither woman was looking for the upper hand and their relationship, built on tenderness and respect, was a model to those around them. "Few traditional marriages between men and women could achieve that level of support and longevity," added Malitte Matta.

During the 1950s, Toto rekindled many of her past friendships. She regularly spent time with Nina Mdivani, Bettina Bergery, Lee Miller, Elisabeth Eichmann, Caresse Crosby, Gala Barbisan and Randolph Churchill and widened her circle of friends on both sides of the English Channel. "I met Toto and Erica in 1956 through Raymond Queneau's wife," remembers Raoul Tubiana. "I saw them in Paris, but mostly in London where, in my capacity as a surgeon, I attended meetings at the Hand Club; I enjoyed spending time with them, at their home or at the gallery, and we became good friends. Erica was rather masculine, a little rough, with an uncanny eye and flair for painting. I admired her tremendously. And I was very drawn to Toto; she was so beautiful and witty, but I could sense there was another, very different, side to her. One was almost completely taken in by her charm. She was secretive and her mysterious past was slightly disturbing. I have never met a woman as enigmatic and unusual."

In Paris, the couple stayed in an apartment on rue de l'Université that was generously loaned to them by gallery owner Heinz Berggruen. Pierina de Gavardie, a close friend and private art dealer, and her daughter, Gianna Sistu, lived in the same building. The four saw each other every day. Sistu recalled, "My mother and I loved them. They would come over for breakfast and always told incredible stories because they really lived in a different universe, far from what we consider to be the real world. I was very young and gained their confidence. They often took me along on their escapades and it was with them that I first visited Alberto Giacometti's studio—an unforgettable memory."

She continued, "Watching them so closely, I could see that Erica was much more in love than Toto was, and that Erica was really terrified at the thought that Toto might ever leave her. Indeed, everyone was fascinated by Toto's aura of mystery and absolute sense of freedom. She gave free rein to her sexuality and always spoke frankly and directly, yet she remained elusive and certain parts of her life were off-limits, a combination that made her unique and irresistible. She was a splendid, radiant creature. I can still picture her walking down the Rue de l'Université, catching the eye of all the passersby who were struck by her allure. Today, nothing is really surprising, but back then Toto and Erica formed a most original couple. They lived together openly, without the slightest embarrassment at a time when most homosexuals concealed their true orientation. Being around them, I really came to understand the meaning of freedom."

In Paris, Toto met several of Erica's longtime French friends, mostly writers. They dined with Raymond Queneau and his wife, Michel Leiris and André Pieyre de Mandiargues. Gala Barbisan introduced Toto to many prominent Parisian hostesses and Toto gained entry to Suzanne Tézenas's salon where she met Emil Cioran, Pierre Boulez and Jean-Louis Barrault. She also accompanied Erica to the studios of Serge Poliakoff and César—both represented by the Hanover Gallery— and attended haute couture fashion shows.

In England, Toto's closest friends were three gay dandies. The first member of this inner circle was Robert Heber-Percy, known as the "Mad Boy." Born into an aristocratic family, he lived at Faringdon, the home of his companion, Lord Berners. Faringdon was the basis for Merlinford in Nancy Mitford's novel *The Pursuit of Love*. After Berners's death in 1950, Heber-Percy remained in the house until his own death in 1987. Strolling in the gardens, guests came across pink flamingos that were fed shrimp to maintain their coloring, as well as pigeons that Heber-Percy had dyed in rainbow shades with vegetable-based paint. He welcomed his guests with parrots perched on his shoulder and often roamed through the ground floor of the house stark naked and on horseback.

Heber-Percy could be wildly generous or mercilessly cruel, and his violent mood swings justified his
nickname. He enjoyed Toto's company and the feeling
was mutual. Miss K. spent many weekends at Faringdon
and met the Mad Boy for lunch whenever he came to
London. Francis Bacon was one of his lovers, a fact that
always amused Toto.

The second member was Neil Munro Roger, or
"Bunny," a former war hero who ran the couture depart-
ment at Fortnum & Mason, one of the city's most ven-
erable establishments. Bunny and his brothers formed
a wild threesome who indulged in every extravagance.
They once attended a costume ball dressed as the Brontë
sisters. Their Walton Street home featured a fresco enti-
tled *Garden of Eden in the Highlands*—a nod to their Scottish
origins—and was the setting for memorable costume
balls that Toto loved to attend. Everyone appreciated
Bunny's hospitality and wit, but some thought he used
too much rice powder; as he aged, his pallid face looked
more and more like a death mask.

The third member was the Honorable Kensington
Davison, the future Lord Broughshane III. The former
Royal Air Force pilot was also a World War II hero who
had bombed Third Reich military bases and devised a
system to jam the enemy's radar. In 1945, his squadron
shot down 278 planes, an accomplishment that earned
him the highest honors. At the end of the conflict,
Ken, as he was known, was sent to Berlin to question

German scientists about their work. He spoke German fluently and was able to obtain crucial information about their research on the atomic bomb.

After his demobilization, Davison worked in the oil industry and civil aviation but it was as director of the Friends of Covent Garden that he left his strongest mark on the London cultural scene. Davison and Toto shared a love of opera, ballet and music and attended every new production. They had much in common—a passion for travel, an ironic sense of humor and a taste for incongruous situations. "Ken claimed it was impossible to be bored for one second in Toto's company. He adored her eccentricity," recalls Lady Deirdre Curteis. "He loved to talk about a particular trip they had taken together, when he accompanied Toto to Tangiers. She was bringing cash to Francis Bacon and they had agreed to meet in a brothel at noon. As they arrived, a bell rang, signaling the lunch hour, and the ladies of the establishment rushed from their rooms, walking out on their clients in the middle of the action! This was exactly the sort of situation that delighted Toto and Ken."

Kensington Davison quickly became Toto's best friend and most devoted admirer, and no man would ever be closer to her. He remained steadfastly by her side until her death.

27

On October 17, 1958, Francis Bacon had a letter delivered to the Hanover Gallery. Michael Greenwood, one of Brausen's assistants, opened the letter and learned that the painter had decided to leave the Hanover for the Marlborough Fine Art gallery. Bacon didn't mention it in the letter, but he had signed a contract with the new gallery one day earlier. Brausen was in Paris at the time, in preparation for the gallery's important summer exhibition and Bacon had shown neither the courage nor the courtesy of announcing his decision to her in person. She was devastated by the news and immediately returned to London. At first, Brausen considered arbitration through the justice system, but in the end, she decided that artists should not be sued and gave up the idea. She would never recover from the blow of his ingratitude.

As incredible as it may seem today, Bacon had never signed a contract with the Hanover Gallery. Breaking a gentlemen's agreement would characterize him as a boor, but nothing more. With no judicial risk involved, Bacon broke with Brausen. His new gallery could advance him much larger sums of money and that appeared to be his main concern. Though Bacon was often cast in the role of a suffering artist who didn't care about material contingencies, he was managing his career with the effectiveness of a gladiator.

The situation was all the more unfair, as Brausen had done everything to promote his work and uphold his reputation for more than ten years. "Bacon was Erica," concluded Brausen's friend Edmonde Charles-Roux who, at the time, was editor-in-chief of the influential French *Vogue*. When Bacon's work had been met with only revulsion and a lack of understanding, Brausen fervently supported the artist, advancing him as much money as she could while his many unsold paintings sat in the basement.

Brausen established Bacon's reputation in England and abroad. Thanks to Brausen, Bacon had his first one-man show in Paris a few months earlier, in 1957, at Jean Lacarde. She had put up with his impossible behavior—he would deliver paintings that were still wet on the day of an opening, causing her immeasurable stress. Bacon's paintings would eventually fetch astronomical prices, but that did not happen for many years. Of all his exhibitions at the Hanover Gallery, only the Van Gogh series was successful financially, and for the wrong reason: Vincente Minnelli had just directed a film about Van Gogh starring Kirk Douglas. After so much effort on Brausen's part, another gallery was going to reap the rewards of her work and finally profit from Bacon's success.

Toto flew to Brausen's side, supporting and comforting her as best she could. She took Brausen to Covent Garden to see *Boris Godunov* and *Der Rosenkavalier,* planned dinners with Michel Leiris, surrealist painter André Masson and their devoted friends Peter Brook and Natasha Parry. After spending many evenings together, Toto and Erica went to Paris to celebrate Christmas with Gala Barbisan.

In early January 1959, when Toto felt that Brausen was ready to return to work and remain in London on her own, Toto went on holiday to Kitzbühel, an elegant ski resort in the Austrian Tyrol. There, Toto met a woman who would become one of her dearest friends. Lady Grantley, known today as Lady Deirdre Curteis, was young enough to be Toto's daughter, but the two women quickly developed a strong connection.

"Toto was fascinating. I had never met anyone quite like her, casually or intimately. I was in my twenties and had led a very sheltered life, a far cry from the life she had known. Toto was an exceptional storyteller and that talent was reinforced by her lively delivery. She spoke English without any trace of an accent, but she would invent words and use unusual expressions that added a delicious flavor to her conversation. Beneath the humor and the vivaciousness, she was a truly a loyal and courageous person whose candor was baffling in those buttoned-up times. She had none of Erica's edginess that often reminded me of Oscar Wilde's Lady Bracknell. The couple did not go unnoticed, I can assure you. At the same time, Toto was very discreet, never speaking of her past but always willing to answer any question even if it pertained to the atrocities she underwent during the war. Out of modesty or courtesy, nobody dared to ask her about the espionage and the Resistance—which was unfortunate because I am sure that she would have answered."

When they returned to London, Toto and Lady Curteis met again at the home of their mutual friend Sir Philip Dunn, at Stowell Park in Wiltshire. She said, "We really got to know each other during that first weekend. At the time, Toto was enthralled with archaeology; it had become her passion. She had just returned from an expedition with Seton Lloyd and was reading everything on the subject. From that point on, we saw each other very often."

The year 1959 marked a pivotal moment for Toto and Erica. The Hanover Gallery organized its last

Francis Bacon exhibition—the painter did not attend the opening—and the two women were about to embark on an exciting new project. After founding an art gallery together, they had decided to buy property on a Sicilian island.

28

On January 21, 1959, Toto and Erica received a letter
from one of their friends, Italian painter Leonardo
Cremonini. Enclosed with the letter was a photograph
that immediately caught their attention—it depicted a
property for sale on Panarea, one of the Aeolian Islands
in the Tyrrhenian Sea, north of Sicily. Cremonini
compared the place to paradise and urged them to con
sider it seriously.

Toto flew to Italy a few days later to inspect the
property. After a short stopover in Milan, where she
attended a performance of Prokofiev's *Romeo and Juliet* at
La Scala, Miss K. arrived in Panarea on February 27.
The trip from Naples to Panarea aboard a run-down
boat was an expedition in itself: the boat left the port at
7:30 P.M. and did not arrive in Panarea until 1:00 P.M.
the following day.

Located between Lipari and Stromboli, Panarea is a tiny island with a surface measuring 1.3 square miles. Although it had been inhabited since the 14th century B.C.E., there were no roads, only mule tracks and virtually no beaches—one had to climb down the rocks to reach the sea. The wild terrain featured typical Mediterranean vegetation—prickly pear trees, broom and caper shrubs and olive trees. Toto instantly fell in love with its volcanic topography and contacted Erica, who decided to buy the property straight away.

Toto remained in Panarea to oversee the construction project, as the only building on the property was a run-down house. She stayed in the island's only café-hotel and worked tirelessly with the help of their friend Malitte Matta, who had purchased a house on the island one year earlier with her husband, Chilean painter Roberto Matta. Malitte Matta recalled, "Toto took charge of the building project, hired the contractors and personally supervised the construction work. She was surprisingly efficient, especially for a woman who projected such a sophisticated image. We were light-years away from the openings at the Hanover."

Toto studied the style of local construction to avoid anachronisms and worked closely with the architect and other tradesmen. She also went to Sicily to buy doors, windows, tables, dressers and beds from local antique dealers and flea markets. She brought back antique painted sacristy furniture, terra cotta ovens, including one shaped like a goddess with her arm raised, dishes and yards of fabric.

Panarea had neither water nor electricity, but nothing could deter Toto's frenzied work. She even designed terraced gardens that descended toward the sea. As the volcanic soil was sterile, Miss K. brought in soil and fertilizer from the mainland and did the planting herself. She chose jasmine, bougainvillea and tobacco flowers, creating a harmony of colors. In order to irrigate the plants, Toto had to rely on reservoir-boats that traveled from island to island. She became their best customer.

The construction work would take years, but the place began to take shape after just a few months. Erica, who had first come in March, was amazed to discover the transformations that had taken place when she returned in July 1959. Toto and Erica's first guest, in August of the same year, was Elisabeth Eichmann, who said, "Panarea was entirely conceived by Toto. It was a magical place. She had designed everything around the light. The rooms were very airy with immaculate white walls; the only splashes of color, inside and out, came from flowers or pillows. It was both simple and elegant."

Over time, Toto built six cottages and an actual hamlet and christened the property Le Case dei Sette Mulini or The Houses of the Seven Windmills. "It was a complete success and the garden was enchanting, one of the most beautiful of its kind. Toto had a true sense of luxury, real luxury, very spare, very pure, a far cry from the extravagances of the nouveaux riches. She had original and unique ideas when it came to decorating and Erica paid for everything. Toto was expensive," explained Edmonde Charles-Roux, who visited Panarea every summer for close to fifteen years.

F.C. agreed that "Erica took on the role of Mrs. Sisyphus, who did the work, while Toto played Miss Danaide and did the spending... Of course, you had to admit that Toto had created a true masterpiece in Panarea, a folly, in the 18th-century sense of the word, and right next to Stromboli, an active volcano. Erica was very proud of her."

While their friends noticed Erica's endless generosity toward Toto, some of them saw it in a different light: "Toto was her true love and she would go to any lengths to please her, that was for sure," declared Malitte Matta. "Still, Panarea, which quickly became a prestigious destination, was an extraordinary showcase for Erica. She invited artists, collectors, museum directors and art critics and Toto, always the perfect hostess, welcomed them lavishly. The guests mingled with their friends and the confluence of personalities and ideas was unquestionably beneficial for the Hanover."

Today, Panarea is unrecognizable and overrun by tourists, but when Toto conceived her Xanadu, it was an arid and poetic place whose essence was perfectly captured by Roberto Rossellini in *Stromboli* and by Michelangelo Antonioni in *L'Avventura*. Toto loved her many roles: master builder, landscape artist, hostess and, when the need arose, plumber, for herself or her neighbors. Miss K., who had never been listless or lethargic, took great pleasure in overcoming nature's obstacles and battling the elements for the sake of beauty.

"If you have a garden and a library, you have everything you need," said Cicero. Toto always arrived in Panarea with suitcases filled with novels and essays, and she spent hours there reading, surrounded by her flowers. After having lived so many years in an urban environment, she could spend weeks at a time on her own, without any company, and derived great happiness from the island's peaceful lifestyle.

29

The cycle that began with Francis Bacon's departure
and the building project in Panarea took a new turn
when, in late 1959, Erica and Toto decided to move out
of the Boltons apartment they had shared since 1946.

They set their sights on a duplex, located on the
third and fourth floors of a building at 70 Eaton
Place. Their choice of address could not have been
more elegant, and the new apartment's quirky layout—
unexpected nooks and a narrow interior staircase—
enchanted them instantly. They bought a leasehold
interest, as was customary in London. To come up with
the necessary funds, Brausen sold her last six works by
Bacon to the Marquess of Dufferin and Ava, whose
mother, Maureen, had long been friends with Toto.

After moving in, Toto and Erica spared no expense
in decorating the apartment; once again, Erica gave Toto
carte blanche. They ordered furniture and fixtures—

specifically, four armchairs, two stools, two chandeliers, two lamps and a coffee table, all in bronze—from their good friends Alberto and Diego Giacometti. The combination of these pieces with the Empire and Biedermeier chairs and bureaus that Erica favored and the paintings she brought home—as she had done in the Boltons apartment—created a refined and unusual atmosphere that often startled their guests.

"It was a touch extreme for the British," recalled Lady Deirdre Curteis with a smile. "The result was very theatrical and certainly unlike anything you would see in London at the time. The Giacometti furniture . . . an original concept, but nothing could be less comfortable!" Raoul Tubiana remembered "a place that was both stylish and unusual. It was the first time I had seen furniture made of bronze, but what was most memorable was the quality of the paintings displayed on the living room walls."

Throughout the years, Brausen bought paintings that she could only keep for a short time. Because of her constant need for money, she was always eventually compelled to sell them. In the Boltons apartment where the couple moved in 1946 and then in the apartment on Eaton Place, Toto lived in a virtual museum, even if the works of art came and went according to the women's financial needs. At some point, Brausen had owned Francis Bacon's *Painting*, Henri Matisse's *The Red Studio*, Pierre Bonnard's *L'Été*, Georges Rouault's *Le*

Christ aux Outrages, Joan Miró's *L'Âne au Potager* and a piece by Paul Klee, her favorite, an image of squares and tufts of grass. "It was always exciting to receive an invitation from Erica and Toto, because you never knew what extraordinary surprise awaited you," recalled Tubiana.

The women's bedrooms reflected their respective personalities. Toto had selected black and garnet wallpaper that resembled Persian mosaics, gold leaf for the ceiling and a sienna earth tone for the door. A beautiful drawing by Amedeo Modigliani—depicting a seated woman, with her legs folded under her—and her favorite books completed the room's décor. The housekeeper was instructed to have a fresh bouquet of roses on display at all times, and those roses were purchased exclusively from Miss K.'s favorite flower shop located in Victoria Station. Brausen's choice of design was more in line with a younger woman's taste—white walls, a watercolor by Marie Laurencin and a vase created by Alberto Giacometti for Elsa Schiaparelli in the 1930s.

The Eaton Place apartment and the Panarea property represented the ideal confluence of intelligence, fine taste and affluence. The guests were equally scintillating: Jean Tinguely and Niki de Saint Phalle, two artists who had become friends, Alexander Calder and Serge Poliakoff, writers Raymond Queneau and Cyril Connolly, directors Peter Brook and Luchino Visconti, eccentric characters—the Mad Boy, Nina Mdivani, Gala Barbisan and Bunny Roger, contemporary music composer Pierre Barbaud, architect Ernö Goldfinger, archaeologist Max Mallowan and Toto's close friend, Princess Ekaterina Pavlovich Galitzine, a Russian grande dame married to Englishman John Campbell. Erica and Toto were gracious hostesses, and people were delighted to gather at Eaton Place for cocktails at the end of the day. When Erica and Toto gave small dinners, they took turns doing the cooking.

When they were not entertaining, the couple rarely spent the evening at home together. If Toto was the hare, Erica was the tortoise. Toto could not remain idle and she was either out every night or traveling. Erica, on the other hand, was very sedentary and preferred to remain at home, where she studied cuneiform writing in order to read *The Epic of Gilgamesh* in the original. She was fascinated by the story of the King of Uruk, the hero of ancient Mesopotamia, and she was eventually able to decipher the Sumerian texts that recounted the king's adventures. Erica was also interested in esoteric architecture and its secrets. She believed the Tour Saint-Jacques in Paris and Stonehenge in England, where she went for the occasion of the winter solstice, represented an elevated form of spirituality.

"Erica justified Toto's constant travels because of her love of music. Toto toured Europe to attend the performances of renowned orchestra leaders and famous soloists," remembered Gianna Sistu. Still, Miss K. was present whenever she was needed. "I always had the impression that Erica depended on Toto's support, and Toto would return to London to be at her side for all the important openings at the Hanover. She seemed lost without Toto. Erica was never interested in music as Toto was; from the late 1920s until her death, Toto was a true connoisseur of opera—from its arias and casting to the staging and orchestration. Erica admired her extensive knowledge on the subject," remembered F.C.

Their friends believed Erica accepted Toto's absences and whims because of what Toto had been through during the war. When traveling by train or plane, Toto could never sit anywhere but on the aisle, because she was very claustrophobic. "Ravensbrück," Brausen would intone gravely to justify her companion's behavior.

At the time, Miss K.'s schedule was truly staggering. After moving to Eaton Place in 1960, Toto left for Panarea in May. She then went to Naples and Rome before meeting Erica for the Biennale in Venice, where they dined with their friend and client Peggy Guggenheim. Toto returned to Panarea on her own before flying back to Rome to hear Mstislav Rostropovich play Prokofiev. From there, she traveled to Paris, Vienna and back to London before returning again to Paris, where Gala Barbisan introduced her to Nathalie Sarraute and Michel Butor. Finally, after a weekend in Faringdon with the Mad Boy, Toto and

Erica spent Christmas in Paris before heading back to London for a New Year's Eve celebration at Bunny Roger's home, where Toto arrived on the arm of Ken Davison. While this lifestyle suited Toto perfectly, Erica soon tired of it and suffered more and more from Toto's repeated absences.

30

The most significant periods of Toto's life were spent on three different islands. First, there was Java, where the young biracial "green Dutchgirl" developed the taste for mystery and secrecy that would forever be her trademark. Next was England, where she went to shoot a film in which she never appeared, and where the splendid and free-spirited young woman matured into the bold and intimidating woman who was the focus of many scandalous rumors, yet managed to remain bemused by them all. It was in England, too, where, after the war, she helped Erica Brausen establish her gallery before nurturing her own aspirations and earning a degree in archaeology. And soon after her fiftieth birthday, she discovered the third island, Panarea, where she spent her later years in the kind of secluded and exclusive environment that she found so appealing.

"The spirit of these small islands was always established in the same way," explained Edmonde Charles-Roux. "It begins with a painter—Iacovleff in Capri, Cremonini in Panarea—and two or three exceptional women who set about creating a slice of paradise. In Panarea, those women were Toto and Marina Volpi, a sophisticated Venetian aristocrat whose raspy voice was always a surprise. The inseparable neighbors were the very soul of Panarea. The group also included the Mattas, the extraordinary Sicilian jeweler Fulco di Verdura and Luchino Visconti's sister Ida. Panarea was too wild and dangerous for most socialites. There were no cars on the island and the footpaths could prove deadly, especially at night. Walking along the rutted trails might easily result in a broken ankle. Unlike Capri, there were no chic yachts on which one went to be seen. Panarea attracted a small group of creative and free-minded people—an atmosphere that owed a great deal to Toto Koopman. In the 1960s, no place was more elegant than Panarea. Its absolute simplicity was the direct opposite of the circus-like atmosphere of Capri."

Marina Volpi was the daughter of Giuseppe Volpi, the founder of the Venice International Film Festival She divided her time between the Aeolian Islands and the Villa Barbaro, her home in Maser—built by Palladio and decorated with frescoes by Veronese—where Toto had been a guest on several occasions. Miss K. was aware that British guests were often surprised by her friend's eccentric hospitality, which mixed the grandiose with a touch of morbidity. "In Panarea, she would take us to visit Marina, who lived nearby, and we would listen to Puccini and watch the sun set into the sea," recalled Lady Deirdre Curteis. "There was a three-legged dog who added a note of typically Italian humor, disconcerting and grotesque at the same time."

Toto and Marina were Panarea's appointed hostesses during the summer. They had to work around the schedule of each resident, as many were involved with their own projects. Matta and Cremonini painted, taking advantage of the intense afternoon sunlight; Fulco di Verdura designed his jewelry collections; Luchino Visconti worked on a film script; and Edmonde Charles-Roux was writing a biography of Chanel. "Toto recognized that while we were a group of happy vacationers, we also devoted time to our work," recalled Charles-Roux. "She was respectful of every household's privacy, as each one had its own groups of friends. Sometimes there was friction and cooling-off periods between the groups, but that was all part of the game, and reconciliations were always colorful. Everyone went swimming separately, for privacy, and usually gathered in the evenings. Toto understood all of that very well. She was wonderful when Gaston Defferre stayed with me every year, and he appreciated her consideration. At the time, Gaston was mayor of Marseilles, and he did not want to be disturbed during the day so that he could rest and work in peace. Toto would decide where we would meet at the end of the afternoon, around 6:00 P.M. We would get together at each other's homes, and she managed the logistics beautifully. Toto was very intuitive, very psychological, much more so than Erica ever was—more cerebral and intellectual."

Miss K. oversaw every single detail at Le Case dei Sette Mulini, starting with the lunches and dinners that usually involved twelve guests. When the food supply was low, Toto didn't hesitate to hail fishermen from on board the Matta's boat, pleading with them to sell her some fish—which they eventually did, at a handsome price. She also made sure that Erica, whose liver had been severely damaged by a serious case of jaundice, always ate the appropriate foods. Her dietary restrictions allowed her only boiled carrots, white rice and fresh compotes. "That was sheer madness, because vegetables, fruits, butter, milk and cheese were all brought in from Naples and cost them a fortune," recounted F.C. "One day, I calculated that it would cost them less to live at the Ritz and order anything they wanted. Erica went through all the money from the gallery, money that she had worked so hard to earn over the years. Furthermore, as there were no actual beaches, they had to pay fishermen a fee of 15,000 lire per hour to escort their guests by boat for a swim. But they never spoke about it. Everything ran smoothly, as if it did not matter."

The kitchen was the private domain of one of the fishermen's wives, but Toto often joined her to prepare jars of capers that she gave to her guests as souvenirs. For each meal, she set the tables on the different terraces and decorated them with bouquets of flowers cut from her garden. At nightfall, she set out dozens of elegant glass candle holders, two on each step, reaching down to the sea. "We would have dinner looking out at the erupting Stromboli volcano, I have never seen anything more magical," remembered Elisabeth Eichmann. "The beautiful adventuress of the 1930s and 1940s had become an exemplary hostess," recalled F.C. "I can still picture her, in a caftan, welcoming her elegantly dressed guests, who had walked over from different parts of the island. Edmonde Charles-Roux, arriving for dinner in total darkness, personified the chic spirit of Panarea in a white lace dress and carrying a lantern."

Toto's dinner parties always featured an eclectic mix of guests and scintillating conversation. Ken Davison asking Roberto Matta about his friendship with Fidel Castro; German photographer Willy Maywald exchanging travel stories with composer Pierre Barbaud while Toto and Luchino Visconti compared different opera productions. "She directed the conversation in three or four different languages with incredible ease," remembers Malitte Matta. "It was quite extraordinary to listen to Toto and Luchino talk about music and we would all stop talking so we could listen to them."

Toto and Visconti saw each other often in the 1960s, in Panarea, in Rome and in London, but nobody knew exactly when or where they had first met—perhaps in Italy, through communist members of the Resistance, or in Panarea, through Visconti's sister Ida.

It should be pointed out that many of the visiting artists received commissions for future work and were thrilled. Such was the case for painter Hans Denning, who was commissioned to create a psychedelic portrait of Robert Heber-Percy's dog using multicolored stripes. Some of the artists saw each other again at openings at the Hanover Gallery where they discovered the work of their newfound friends. Collectors, including Robert and Lisa Sainsbury, were regular guests and their patronage was avidly sought.

"Her home was like a ministry of grace," wrote Sainte-Beuve about Princess Mathilde, a cousin of Napoleon III. This was also a fitting description of Le Case dei Sette Mulini. "Toto and Erica's hospitality was the height of civilized living," declared Gianna Sistu. "After the boat trip, the contrast was all the more surprising. We traveled there in overcrowded and dilapidated boats that always seemed to be on the verge of sinking. Everything was run down and there were only two private cabins that could not be reserved. Passengers slept on bunks, six per cabin, while the others had to remain out on the decks, in the open air. Toto and Erica's friends, famous artists and members of the British and Italian aristocracy, along with their mountains of luggage, traveled side by side with Sicilian peasants and their animals. It was quite an adventure, and the trip felt endless as the boat made stops on each of the islands. And then you reached their home, where gardens were irrigated with water brought in from Naples and where you might find yourself seated at dinner between Peter Brook and César. Their only enemy was triviality."

The guests happily embraced the rhythm of life on Panarea. Toto would entertain them with stories about Teresina and Annunziata, the two witches who lived on the island. One could cast the curse of the *malocchio*, the evil eye, while the other one could reverse it, but they regularly switched roles, which kept everyone confused. Panarea also had its own little dictator, and woe to anyone who did not consult him before choosing a house or a piece of property. Not asking his advice turned daily life into a nightmare: boats would forget to deliver goods and mail simply disappeared.

As for the island's only telephone, it belonged to Giovannino, the grocer who lived and worked at the very top of the island. If a call came in from the mainland, he would inform the recipient through his loudspeaker, right from his shop. "Gaston received many calls from Marseilles," recalled Edmonde Charles-Roux, "and Giovannino, who was particularly indiscreet, blared out whatever inquiries were being made on the phone, regardless of their personal or confidential nature. He spoke in Sicilian and I would translate, to the great amusement of the neighbors, but everyone had their turn. Gaston, who was especially fond of Surrealism, adored the typically Panarean ambiance that was the exact opposite of Deauville and Saint-Tropez." Listening to Giovannino's announcements became one of the favorite pastimes of the island's residents.

Sometimes though, cruelty showed its face in the middle of all the enjoyment. "Who can forget the day when Natasha Parry's cat was *assassinated*?" asked Malitte Matta. "That was a real tragedy. Her cat was just like her—beautiful, refined, simply adorable. Of course, he could not roam about freely with all the wild dogs on the island. It just took one minute of distraction, just one, and the poor thing was torn to pieces. Natasha was completely devastated. This woman, who was sweetness personified, had never witnessed such a bloody incident. She and Peter never returned. That was a different side of Panarea."

Over the course of those many summers, Toto and Erica took great pleasure in underwater archaeology. They spent hours exploring the Mediterranean fauna and flora and looking for ship wreckage. The bond that existed between them amazed their friends. "They were so natural together," remembered Edmonde Charles-Roux. " In a world so full of complexity, here were two women who loved each other so easily and with such spontaneity. They were remarkably intelligent, each in her own way, but at the same time, you could feel that Toto and Erica had experienced tragedy and sadness that the others had not. There had been a frightful past, concentration camps and a great deal of mystery and secrecy related to espionage. They were very committed to each other, and I never witnessed a single disagreement between them. They were very protective of each other."

Toto was so enamored of Panarea that she spent more and more time there—so much time that in 1962, she gave up the archaeological expeditions that previously had been so important to her. The beautification of the Panarea property had become an obsession and nothing was beyond reach for Le Case dei Sette Mulini. As always, Erica went along with Toto's wishes, even though it meant that she would have to work even harder to meet her companion's financial needs. For this reason, in 1961, she decided to partner with Peter Gimpel and open a second gallery, this time in Zurich, Switzerland.

31

While the impact of "swinging London" reverberated around the world, the Hanover Gallery and the fascinating artists it represented were transforming the way generations of British people viewed and appreciated art. "It was a place where the creative spirit was always alive and where one could see the most brilliant artwork of the time," concluded Peter Brook. Over the years, the gallery's exhibits included sculptor Louise Nevelson's stacked boxes, Jean Dubuffet's *L'Hourloupe*—a series of drawings done with a ballpoint pen—César's *Compressions Dirigées*, Eva Aeppli's bronze and textile figurines and, thanks to a collaboration between Brausen and the Denise René Gallery in Paris, examples of Kinetic art.

Victor Vasarely pioneered the Kinetic movement, a geometric art form that played with optical illusions. Hans Arp and Yaacov Agam also contributed to the movement. Intrigued by their research, Brausen was the first to exhibit their works in London. "I exhibited their work in my gallery and when [Brausen and I] became friends, she also decided to show them," remembers Denise René, nearly fifty years later. "The Hanover was a very high profile venue, very active and stimulating. Erica had an impeccable reputation and painters and sculptors trusted her completely. They always told me she had been instrumental in advancing their careers and that there were never any unpleasant surprises. The artists were paid immediately—a rare occurrence in our circles. And her gallery openings could not have been more brilliant, thanks in great part to Toto. She made the rest of us look provincial."

The Kinetic movement immediately captivated the attention of the art enthusiasts Brausen had cultivated for more than twenty years. Peter Brook was so fascinated by one of the pieces exhibited in "The Movement," a group show at the gallery, that he stopped by to touch it every day. The work in question was *Tactile Painting*, a mural relief by Agam—a black panel with chrome pastilles mounted on springs. When Luchino Visconti came to visit Toto at the gallery, he discovered Vasarely's *Folklore Planétaire*, a series of illustrations assembled in a book. Struck by the work, Visconti immediately bought it as a gift for his latest protégé, Helmut Berger.

During the 1960s, the Hanover was one of swinging London's celebrity destinations. Ordinary visitors might come upon Cecil Beaton shooting photographs of Penelope Tree for *Vogue,* or the elegant Lee Radziwill arriving on the arm of film director Mike Nichols—whose first two films, *Who's Afraid of Virginia Woolf?* and *The Graduate,* had catapulted him to success. They might encounter Russian ballet star Rudolf Nureyev, American industrialist Jean Paul Getty—who was filmed for a television show in the gallery—the Beatles or even Princess Margaret, who dined with Brausen and Toto on three separate occasions in 1963 and 1964.

Toto's eccentric friends could always be counted on to make grand entrances. Though she was now three times her original size, Nina Mdivani wore the latest Courrèges mini-dresses, and her appearance left bystanders speechless. Looking like Ubu the Queen, Nina arrived at the Hanover Gallery for a Dubuffet exhibition in her custom-made beet-colored Rolls-Royce Silver Shadow.[20] Although it was the height of summer, she was wrapped in chinchilla—she claimed she was freezing.

Emerging from under the chinchilla wrap, Nina resembled a giant peony in a cloud of sheer pink chiffon that left little to the imagination. The spectacle was further enlivened by the presence of her third husband, Anthony Harwood. An ailing homosexual, Harwood was the former secretary to Denis Conan Doyle, Nina's second and since deceased husband. He had a pronounced limp and his twisted body resembled an old grapevine. His silver poplin suit matched the chauffeur's uniform. Arm in arm, Toto and Nina chatted happily as they walked around the gallery under the bemused gaze of the other visitors.

Not to be outdone, Miss K. had not relinquished any of her youthful audacity. One day, when someone mentioned her old friend Caresse Crosby and how clever she was for having invented the brassiere, Toto immediately responded, "It's a completely pointless invention. I have never worn one in my entire life, and I have a magnificent bosom." With that, she opened her shirt to reveal her naked breasts, proving beyond any doubt that she was telling the truth. As had been the case throughout her life, her demeanor charmed some and irritated others, but no one could be indifferent to her.

Every month, the public came to the Hanover to see the latest solo or group exhibition. Connoisseurs always made a point of examining one particular display case that featured works that were not part of the current show. On view in the twenty-foot vitrine were Brausen's favorite drawings or small sculptures, perhaps a charcoal drawing by Picasso that the gallery owner had purchased from her friend Alice B. Toklas or a silver *Priapus* by Man Ray. There was always something sure to surprise the interested viewers, and that area of the gallery soon became a meeting place for a new generation of young talented artists such as David Hockney and Bruce Chatwin. Before he began painting his series of California swimming pools, Hockney's work epitomized the best of British pop art. The John Kasmin Gallery had represented him since 1963 but Hockney always liked to visit the Hanover and discover Brausen's latest finds.

Bruce Chatwin met Erica and Toto when he worked as an art expert at Sotheby's, located near the Hanover. In 1966, he left Sotheby's to become a full-time archeologist before writing for the *Sunday Times Magazine*. Chatwin, who enjoyed the company of older women with strong personalities like architect and furniture designer Eileen Gray and fashion designer Madeleine Vionnet, was particularly fond of Erica and Toto. He visited the gallery regularly and was a frequent guest for drinks or dinner on Eaton Place and on Panarea, where he had an open invitation. Toto always spoke admiringly of his first book, *In Patagonia,* published in 1977. She often gave copies of it as gifts to her many friends. "They thought Bruce was perfect," recalled F.C. "He was very handsome, cultured and talented and had a sharp sense of humor... in other words, everything they liked and looked for in a human being. Simple mortals were of no interest to them."

When young admirers asked Erica who her favorite artists were, she would laugh, "You British have the greatest painter of all times... George Stubbs!" Her answer was perplexing because nobody knew whether she was being serious. Wasn't Stubbs known for his portraits of horses?

Sometimes, Erica and Toto's friends were also clients. Peter Brook and Natasha Parry acquired a William Scott; Raoul Tubiana chose a Poliakoff and a double-sided drawing by Giacometti; Philippe de Rothschild selected two paintings by Dubuffet that are still at Mouton today. "They look like two little paintings by Clouet," exclaimed his American-born wife, Pauline. "You could just tuck them into a little raspberry basket!" Philippe promptly bought them.

The Rothschilds and Erica and Toto became friends. When the Rothschilds wanted to have the labels for their vintage wines designed by contemporary painters, Erica was happy to provide them with a list of artists to consider. In return, they always sent Erica and Toto a case of wine at Christmas. The Rothschild hospitality appealed to Toto; it was said that guests at Mouton, in the Bordeaux region, who fell asleep with their hands outside of the covers would awaken to find that their nails had been carefully manicured.

Miss K. tried her best to attract wealthy collectors to the Hanover, but her efforts sometimes fell short. One day, Toto's friend Patrick O'Higgins, a French-Irish journalist, invited her to dinner at the Ritz. O'Higgins was private secretary to Helena Rubinstein and had arranged for Toto to meet the formidable founder of the eponymous cosmetics company. Nearly one hundred years old, and at the head of a considerable fortune, Rubinstein was still actively buying homes, jewelry and works of art.

Toto immediately invited her to visit the Hanover. Brausen, wearing an austere Dior suit, welcomed O'Higgins and Rubinstein to the gallery. Mindful of the caliber of her visitor's private collection, she presented carefully selected drawings, paintings and sculptures, but Rubinstein left without buying anything. Brausen, who was perpetually anguished over money issues, remained impassive, never letting her disappointment show.

The Hanover pampered its artists. After each opening, Brausen would host a dinner in an elegant restaurant such as Annabel's, one of London's most exclusive nightclubs. Only members were admitted to the club, but Toto was able to convince a friend to make a reservation in his name. The ruse worked and, of course, Brausen paid for the entire evening's entertainment. Brausen made it a point to meet painters or sculptors at the airport. As she waited, champagne in hand, to greet Louise Nevelson, she exclaimed, "Americans don't realize that they have their own Brancusi!" Talent meant everything to Brausen.

Some professional relationships turned into friendships, and several of Erica's protégés became regular guests at Eaton Place or on Panarea. Jean Tinguely, Niki de Saint Phalle and Alberto Giacometti became close friends, as did the painter Horst Antes. Today, Antes has only fond memories of Erica and, he said, of "Toto, with whom I shared a birthday that we faithfully celebrated together."

Brausen's generosity toward the artists she represented knew no limits. Bryan Robertson, the director of the Whitechapel Gallery, came to see Brausen when he wanted to organize a tribute to Poliakoff. As Brausen was Poliakoff's official agent in England, Robertson asked if she would participate in underwriting the costs of the exhibition. Brausen immediately took out her checkbook and gave him 1,000 pounds, a considerable sum at the time. The spontaneous gesture was typical of her personality and the Poliakoff retrospective at the Whitechapel Gallery was one of London's major events of 1963.

32

From the moment it opened its doors in 1947, the Hanover Gallery was always at the center of important aesthetic developments. Brausen continued to discover and introduce major artists to the British art scene. Today, one expects that level of work, insight and commitment on the part of a gallery, but at the time, it came at a great cost.

Behind the brilliant façade, the groundbreaking work and the openings that quickly turned into happenings lay the bitter reality of Brausen's ongoing financial struggles. She received no outside support, not even from the press. Neither of Niki de Saint Phalle's first two exhibitions in London received any coverage. It was the same for the Tinguely exhibition, yet Brausen continued to support them through the difficult times. And there was the matter of the unsold works. Brausen was in possession of more than eighty pieces by Giacometti and it would take her ten years to sell them. She also exhibited the work of Henry Moore, whose spectacular bronze pieces were difficult to sell. Louise Nevelson's works were equally challenging. And the list goes on.

Brausen also had to contend with the whims of the collectors who were her main source of income. Collectors could be shockingly inconsiderate, but Brausen never spoke up for fear of losing their business. Donald Ogden Stewart and his wife were a perfect example of the complexity of these situations. A victim of the witch-hunt against Communist sympathizers in the United States, Donald was a member of the Algonquin Round Table and a brilliant Hollywood screenwriter who moved to London and became one of the Hanover's most important clients.

A close friend of Ernest Hemingway—he was the inspiration for the Bill Gorton character in *The Sun Also Rises*—Ogden was so vocal in his support of the Soviet Union that President Roosevelt is said to have started each day asking for "orange juice, coffee and the first ten telegrams of protest against DOS." Ogden's wife, the journalist Ella Winter, brought to mind the Tracy Lord character in *The Philadelphia Story*, a film for which her husband won an Academy Award. The couple's eccentric behavior even involved the paintings they bought from the Hanover Gallery. When Brausen and Toto visited the Ogdens in their Hampstead home, they discovered that Ella had painted over a Miró and a Mondrian because she found the faded and peeling colors depressing. Brausen was aghast but said nothing. The sacrilegious gesture was just one of the many idiosyncrasies of the rich collectors upon whom she depended.

Brausen also had to contend with the betrayals that were inherent to the art world and her name was sometimes unfairly tarnished. Pierre Matisse, a friend and gallery owner, had purchased what he thought was a bust by Giacometti. He acquired it in Rome with the understanding that it had come from the Hanover, but upon his arrival in New York, he discovered, after measuring it, that the sculpture's dimensions differed by one centimeter from its original size. Further investigation revealed that this particular statue had been previously purchased by another London dealer for a client in Rome. But the statue Matisse bought from the Italian was not the original. Enraged and embarrassed even to be implicated in the story, Brausen testified on behalf of Matisse when he brought suit in a court of law. Brausen was vindicated and her reputation remained intact. There were instances of mutilated and counterfeit sculptures, good and bad forgeries of paintings, suspicious attributions. All dealers have faced these tribulations at one time or another.

A more serious episode tainted Brausen's friendship with Germaine Richier, an artist she had long admired. A former student of Antoine Bourdelle, Richier was known for her "hybrid statues," with bodies that were half human and half vegetable; she often inserted pieces of colored glass and tree branches into her statues. Brausen organized Richier's first one-woman show in England and took on the costs of transporting the monumental pieces in order to introduce her work to the British public. She also acquired *La Feuille*, a statue of a very slender woman with leaf-print patterns. Brausen would eventually have to sell it when she was short of funds.

Shortly before her death in 1959, Germaine Richier envisioned another sculpture, *La Femme à la Colombe*. A Swiss millionaire who was close to both Richier and Brausen commissioned three numbered editions of the statue—"one for Germaine, one for you and one for me." The art patron contacted a foundry in the Swiss canton of Ticino. When Brausen was once again facing financial difficulties, she had to part with her sculpture. She exhibited it in her Zurich gallery, the Gimpel-Hanover, where it quickly sold to a textile industrialist. Six years later, after Germaine Richier's death, the industrialist burst into the gallery and shouted at the director, Anne Rotzler, "Ms. Brausen is a thief and there are many more than three versions of *La Femme à la Colombe*!"

The mystery was quickly solved. The Swiss art collector who had commissioned the work had simply forgotten to have the original plaster mold destroyed. The owner of the foundry, who was a swindler, took advantage of the situation and had made additional copies of the statue.

Brausen immediately went to Zurich. "I am not a thief. How much do you want?" she offered. The wronged client, who had initially paid 4,000 pounds, demanded 40,000 pounds, and Brausen paid that price.

Rotzler was livid. "You never should have done that!" she said. "Take him to court. Why should you pay for someone else's dishonesty?"

"My reputation is worth at least 40,000 pounds," snapped Brausen, barely containing her rage.

Over the next few years, Toto often accompanied Brausen as she divided her time between the two galleries. Brausen personally supervised installations in Zurich, and the couple attended all the openings. "One day, when the three of us were in Switzerland for an exhibition, I learned that Barbara was going to be performing at a theater in Geneva and, thinking they would be pleased—Erica was a close friend of Marianne Oswald and Suzy Solidor—I was able to secure very good seats.[21] It turned out to be one of the worst experiences of my life," recounted F.C. "Erica and Toto disliked her voice to such a point that they wanted to leave in the middle of the show. I convinced them to stay but after the performance, they spoke me in an icy tone:

'Darling, what a delightful evening, so nice of you to have thought of us!' I felt as if I had been pierced with a bayonet." The two women could be vicious—when displeased, they were deadlier than an execution squad.

Over the years many people were subjected to Brausen's harshness. "She could be unspeakably difficult and curt," recalled art historian Fausta Squatriti who regularly contributed to the Hanover's catalogues. "I saw Erica in London, at the gallery, and she no longer was the pleasant and relaxed woman I had known on Panarea," confirmed Edmonde Charles-Roux. "She was scathing with everybody."

Brausen's irritability was the result of too many responsibilities: running two galleries at the same time, finding money for her artists, maintaining Toto's lifestyle in both London and Panarea, as well as subsidizing her many trips. The constant pressure would finally take its toll. In addition, Brausen was increasingly unable to tolerate Toto's sexual escapades. When Toto became infatuated with a Sicilian carabiniere, whom we will call Marco, Brausen could no longer hide how hurt she was. "Erica was falling apart. I remember seeing her in tears. There was always this terror of losing Toto, of seeing her find happiness with someone else," remembered Gianna Sistu.

For Toto, this virile young man—who was clearly harmless, according to everyone who met him—was a lover whose vigor and sensuality fulfilled her needs, and nothing more. She did not see anything wrong with the relationship, and it went on for years, since Erica could always count on Toto's presence when needed, so Toto's relationship with Marco in no way broke the rules of their implicit pact in her mind. Toto was so oblivious to the extent of Erica's weakened state that she even invited Marco to London, where he moved into the Eaton Place guest room.

Yet another upheaval awaited Erica. The passing of Jane Heap in 1964 sounded the death knell for the delicate inner balance she had maintained for twenty years. At some point, she started using drugs. Nobody could say when with certainty, but her dependence grew to the point where she always had a bag filled with syringes on hand. Gianna Sistu said, "We all knew Erica used drugs. She suffered moments of deep depression followed by great highs, and at times she seemed on the edge of hysteria. It was truly heartbreaking, but she was beyond our help." Brausen found unscrupulous doctors who were willing to write prescriptions for morphine.

In May 1968, Brausen's physical state had deteriorated to the point where she had to have stomach surgery for a serious ulcer, further complicating the liver problems that had plagued her for years. Toto took her place at the gallery for several days before leaving on yet another trip with her carabiniere. Toto and Marco drove from Naples to Rome, where Toto introduced him to her good friend, actress Isa Miranda. She traveled to Düsseldorf, to Paris and to Marrakech and, some time later, even managed to spend an entire month in the Soviet Union at a time when that was a most difficult thing to do. She embarked on the long journey from Moscow to Samarkand without Brausen, who once again had stayed behind in London.

In the early 1970s, Brausen was too weary to go on. As an art dealer, she felt she had accomplished her life's work, and the newest art trends no longer excited her. The relentless financial pressures played an important part in her decision to retire.

"Erica never had the soul of an accountant," stated F.C. "When dealing with Bacon, Giacometti or César, she simply gave in, and that was her strength. If she admired something, she yielded. While other gallery owners negotiated percentages, she never did. Her only barometer was her passion." After twenty-six years, the Hanover Gallery closed its doors on April 1, 1973, shortly after Brausen celebrated her sixty-fifth birthday.

33

The Hanover years were synonymous with hard work, hope and disillusionment, success and failure but never monotony. Erica and Toto's lives had been a thrilling whirlwind of fascinating encounters, exhibitions and travel. Each month, guests crowded into the gallery for the newest opening, and the two women's daily routine revolved around this hectic schedule. Suddenly, they were faced with quiet and solitude. Now that they were no longer of use to artists and the social crowd, their phone hardly rang.

For a time, Brausen continued to work with the Gimpel-Hanover Gallery in Zurich and conducted business from her Eaton Place home, trying as best she could to dispose of the works she had kept in reserve. "Erica was selling off the last bits of the Hanover to make a little money, and I tried to help her as much as possible by putting her in touch with specialized buyers," said Gianna Sistu, who had opened her own gallery in Paris. "It was heartbreaking to see her struggling this way after having reigned over the European contemporary art scene for so many years."

Toto helped Erica through this bitter time, sustaining her with tenderness and patience. "After the Hanover closed, Erica was in a constant state of irritation," recalled Lady Deirdre Curteis. "It was hard on Toto, but she never complained. She was completely devoted to her and took wonderful care of Erica during that period." Unlike Erica, who had very few social relationships, Toto always had the support of her closest friends—Deirdre, Ken and the Mad Boy in England and Elisabeth in Vienna.

As soon as the two women could, they sought refuge in Panarea. Underwater explorations were no longer feasible because of Brausen's declining health, but she found comfort in the simple beauty of the island. They sat in the sun, played canasta, had lunch and dinner with friends on the island and spent time reading in the garden. Toto's reading list reveals a great deal about her remarkable personality: travel essays by Patrick Leigh Fermor, *Memories of an Idealist* by Malwida von Meysenbug—the feminist, friend of Wagner and Romain Rolland who introduced Nietzsche to Lou Andreas-Salomé—Baron Corvo's decadent novels *Hadrian the Seventh* and *Chronicles of the House of Borgia*. She also enjoyed Aldous Huxley's early books—*Crome Yellow* and *Marina di Vezza* reminded her of people she had met years earlier—as well as the works of theologian and paleontologist Pierre Teilhard de Chardin.

"It became increasingly difficult for Erica to walk, as her knees caused her a great deal of pain, but Toto remained as active as ever," recalled Malitte Matta. "I have never encountered anyone as clever, who could solve any practical problem that arose. There was something extraordinary about her resourcefulness, how an elegant hostess could do a better job than the most competent plumber and clearly enjoy doing so. Inside the very seductive envelope was a very capable, very intelligent woman. Her close friends enjoyed putting her to the test and she never failed, whether it involved an iron that required a gas cylinder or a pipe that needed to be unclogged."

Malitte Matta continued, "Talking with her was a joy that never waned over time, and we were friends for forty years. Toto had seen it all, lived it all, the best and the worst, and she had wonderful insight and a great sense of humor. She could make me howl with laughter, and I loved her enthusiasm and her lust for life. Erica was darker, moody, and often difficult. The contrast between them was startling."

The atmosphere on Panarea began to change after the successive deaths of the island's famous residents. Ida Visconti was the first to pass away in 1974, followed by her brother Luchino in 1976, Marina Volpi in 1977 and Fulco di Verdura in 1978. In her letters to Elisabeth Eichmann, Toto remarked sadly that the place had lost its soul. Yachts had replaced the fishing boats and motorbikes had taken over the island's narrow paths. Erica, who complained incessantly of her aches and pains, was of no comfort to Toto—only her flower garden provided solace.

When they returned to London, Toto accompanied Erica on her numerous visits to doctors. The medical specialists for her eyes, ear, stomach, legs—no part of the body was overlooked—had taken the place of the artists, writers and eccentric characters of the past. Toto herself had begun to show signs of slowing down and began wellness treatments at Bad Ragaz where she happily met up with her dear friend Elisabeth Eichmann.

Despite a fuller figure and her somewhat faded beauty, Toto was always mindful of her appearance. In 1985, at the age of seventy-seven, she wore Issey Miyake's designs. Arriving at Covent Garden on the arm of Ken Davison, the tall and regal woman with beautiful silver gray hair made a splendid entrance in the Japanese designer's ingeniously pleated accordion dress.

Over the years, Brausen had undergone several operations—in November 1974, January 1979 and October 1979—and her costly medical care threatened the couple's financial condition. Upon learning of the difficulties facing his former dealer and friend, Francis

Bacon sent her 100,000 pounds, using his Canadian friend Barry Joule as an intermediary. Joule and Toto would eventually become close friends. Bacon reconciled with the two women and even went to visit them on Panarea. "At that point, Bacon was in a bad way. He was mourning the death of his companion, but he appeared much calmer, not given to his usual gratuitous cruelty. To my great surprise, he was absolutely charming with Toto," remembered Malitte Matta.

In the early 1980s, Erica and Toto decided to sell three of the six houses on their Panarea property. It had become difficult for Erica to move about. "Panarea was a perfect place for younger, active people but they were now in their seventies, and Erica was in a pitiful state. It was the right decision" noted F.C. "Just getting to the island in good weather was an epic undertaking, but when there was a storm, it was an ordeal. Erica was no longer up to it."

One last far-fetched rumor that circulated about them suggested that the women had been targeted by the Mafia and threatened with reprisals if they did not agree to sell their houses. "I have heard this crazy rumor," said Malitte Matta. "The fact was that they sold the property to Nunzio Amoroso, a very respectable man who ran a company that was the Italian equivalent of Christofle—selling crystal, porcelain and silver for bridal registries. At the very same time, Nunzio's brother, who actually was a member of the Mafia, had just been arrested in the basement of a house in Palermo, and the whole incident had been nationally televised, causing confusion over the Amoroso name. Toto and Erica sold their properties to the highest bidder, and that was all there was to it; the negotiations took place at my home, over lunch."

The final contract was signed on March 23, 1983, and the transaction put an end to their financial problems. From that point on, Toto would return by herself to the island, where she still owned three other houses. Erica remained in London, because the journey, the rutted paths and the many steps connecting the different terraces had become too much of an obstacle for her weakened legs.

34

For a woman who had led her life with such independence and determination, Toto lived out her last days in tragic passivity. The events leading up to her death had all the elements of a Hitchcock plot. In May 1991, Toto suffered a small stroke, fell and broke her hip. She was rushed to the hospital just in time. "I went to visit her there, and while she was physically diminished, her mind was clear, at least most of the time," recounted Lady Deirdre Curteis. "As soon as Toto was stable, Erica was allowed to take her home. I was in the room with them when they were about to leave and I asked Erica if I could come visit her at Eaton Place. 'I am afraid not!' I can still hear her icy tone. Later, when Ken phoned, Erica told him Toto had died when in fact she was alive. He was absolutely furious."

Elisabeth Eichmann was equally outraged: "I saw Toto at Devonshire Hospital, but once they went home,

Erica would not allow me to visit or speak with her over the telephone while she still had moments of lucidity. Her behavior was unforgivable, it was monstrous of her to cut Toto off from the rest of the world, on the pretext that she was protecting Toto. From whom? From her dearest friends who adored her and who would have done anything for her? I believe that Erica, in a moment of morbidity, finally felt she had Toto to herself and no longer had to share her with anyone."

Once they returned to Eaton Place, Erica placed Toto under the care of her own physician, Victor Ratner. Although his patients included famous people like Princess Alexandra and Elizabeth Taylor, Ratner was reputed to be a fearsome charlatan whose mysterious injections of an unknown substance were supposedly going to regenerate Toto's brain. Toto's friends were horrified. "Ken tried to have him stripped of his medical license; it had happened once before over a sordid story concerning drugs," related Lady Deirdre Curteis. "Ratner fled to Israel before returning to London, where he managed to get reinstated, God only knows how. Erica was behaving irresponsibly and entrusting Toto's care to him was an aberration."

Ken Davison secretly enlisted Barry Joule—whom Brausen despised—to help convince Brausen to hire Lydia Voznesenskaya, a Russian nurse he trusted. In her written testimony, requested by the two men, Voznesenskaya revealed appalling details about Brausen. The nurse met Toto for the first time at Devonshire Hospital prior to caring for her at Eaton Place. She was shocked by Brausen's behavior: Toto's Devonshire Hospital doctors had recommended physical activity and encouraged visits from friends, but Brausen refused to comply.

Brausen, more aggressive than ever, fired Voznesenskaya eight days later, after the nurse expressed concern about Toto being kept in a dark and airless room in the middle of August. In her testimony, Voznesenskaya revealed that whenever Toto was lucid and asked to watch television, Brausen would always answer, "We don't have a television. We can't afford one." What's more, Brausen had rejected the treatments prescribed by the hospital doctors in favor of Victor Ratner's prescriptions. After she was fired, Voznesenskaya alerted Devonshire Hospital and Ken Davison, but it was already too late.

Voznesenskaya asked another nurse, Peter Ford, to replace her as of August 9, after she was dismissed. Like his predecessor, Ford first met Toto at the hospital. Barry Joule and Ken Davison obtained his written testimony, wherein he made further incriminating accusations against Brausen. He claimed never to have seen her at the hospital. The doctors had asked Brausen to stay away because her presence caused the usually calm and relaxed Toto to become very agitated and extremely nervous. Two other nurses, Jackie Carson and Helen Eshutinava, were hired to provide additional help.

Peter Ford was very surprised to learn that only Victor Ratner's recommendations were being followed. Ratner's prescribed treatments plunged Toto into an alarming stupor. Ford was even more astonished when he realized that Ratner had never actually examined Toto. Ford's first meeting with Brausen was equally disturbing. Clearly in the throes of paranoia, she was convinced that all of Toto's friends, as well as the employees of Devonshire Hospital, were after her money. She also told Ford that she had prevented the only living member of the Koopman family, Toto's nephew, Robbert, from visiting his ailing aunt. Ford concluded that Brausen was senile and realized that Toto's fate was entirely in the hands of an unstable woman.

After each visit, Jackie Carson would report to Ford, keeping him apprised of Toto's deteriorating condition and informing him that Ratner had yet to appear. Increasingly volatile, Brausen fired Helen Eshutinava without cause. Ford's concern reached its peak when Brausen gave Toto massive doses of a tranquilizer called Haloperidol. The drug, prescribed by Ratner, caused Toto to decline at an alarming speed.

Toto died on August 27, 1991, around midnight. The night before, Victor Ratner had ordered several strong doses of morphine for her over the telephone. The only time Ratner saw Toto was when he came to sign her death certificate twelve hours after her death. Despite their best efforts, Robbert J.B. Koopman and Ken Davison had not succeeded in rescuing Toto from Erica's grasp.

Then began an even more nightmarish period for Toto's close friends. Erica locked herself in a room with Toto's body and remained there for eight days. Each morning, Rosalina, the Portuguese maid, went to Victoria Station to buy Toto's favorite roses. Erica would then arrange the rosebuds around Toto's neck and lie down alongside her.

"She let me say my goodbyes to Toto, who looked magnificent in her long white nightgown, made of fine cloth, with a hint of red close to her face," recounted F.C. "She looked like a Dutch grande dame from another century, modest and demure the exact opposite of the woman she had been. I don't fault Erica, her adoration for Toto was cultlike, and I believe that she refused to let Toto's friends visit at Eaton Place to spare her from their pity. The body had been carefully treated to slow down decomposition, but British laws were very strict, and after nine days the undertakers were required to collect the remains." F.C. then witnessed a scene of exceptional violence: "Because of rigor mortis and the awkward position of the body at the time of death, they could not fit Toto's body into the casket and they had to break one of her arms with a hammer."

Toto was buried in East Finchley Cemetery, near Jane Heap's grave. During the service, Erica handed a red rose, a symbol of Toto's beauty, to each of those attending the funeral. Erica returned to Eaton Place looking more haggard than ever. "I don't need to live any longer," she whispered in despair.

Epilogue

For the next year and a half, Erica Brausen remained alone in her apartment. She would only leave, and with great difficulty, to see Victor Ratner. Officially, he was administering ozone therapy, a treatment that cost her nearly 750,000 pounds. Today, we know that the corrupt doctor was supplying drug addicts with injections of pethidine, a form of heroin.

Erica Brausen died on December 16, 1992. She was buried near Toto in East Finchley Cemetery. When her death was announced, Lady Deirdre Curteis decided to attend her funeral. "I did it for Toto, whom I loved so much, but also for the memory of the happy times we had spent together in London and in Panarea. It was a way of making peace with Erica. I was brought into a room, where I saw a little old woman whose face appeared joyful and wonderfully serene. As I left, I thought they must have made a mistake: that could not have been Miss Brausen. And yet, it really was Erica! Her customary harsh and hostile frown had vanished. She was finally free of her torment."

Acknowledgments

I wish to express my profound gratitude to the following people and institutions:

Charlotte Aillaud, AIVD (Algemene Inlichtingen-en Veiligheidsdienst or Dutch Intelligence and Security Service), Horst Antes, Élisabeth Barillé, M. Benmiloud (Archives of the Prefecture of Police of Paris), Blanche Blackwell, Leonello Brandolini, Pascaline Bressan, Peter Brook, Edmonde Charles-Roux, Anne Chisholm, John Craxton, Madeleine Dagli, Claude Delay, Jacqueline Demornex, the Dowager Duchess of Devonshire, Marika Genty (and the members of the Conservatoire Chanel), Han Grooten-Feld (Embassy of the Netherlands in Paris), Tammo Hagedoorn, Rana Kabbani, Nelly Kaplan, Nicole Lattès, Marie-Françoise Leclère, Rodolphe Leroy (Raymond Queneau collection at the Université de Bourgogne), the late James Lord, Mary S. Lovell, Claude Makovski, Michael Mallon, Raymond Mason, Malitte Matta, Bernard Minoret, Charlotte Mosley, Musée Galliera (Sylvie Roy and the other librarians), Olivier Nicolas (then the Consul General of France to the Netherlands), Jutta Niemann (Willy Maywald Archives), Malcy Ozannat, Pierre Passebon, Bertrand Pizzin, Alexis Poliakoff, Jean-Marie Queneau, Denise René, John Richardson, Yvonne Robinson-Knapp, Baroness Philippine de Rothschild, Emmanuelle Roederer, Camillo Rospigliosi, Gianna Sistu, Fausta Squatriti, John Stefanidis, Danièle Thompson, the late Denise Tual, Raoul Tubiana.

In Vienna, I wish to thank Elisabeth Eichmann, one of Toto Koopman's closest friends, for her infinite kindness. She answered my many queries and trusted me with several of Toto's letters. For this, I can never thank her enough.

In London, Lady Deirdre Curteis enlightened me about the unique character of her dear friend Toto. I gained enormous insight through our correspondence, which lasted many months while I was in Paris and she was in Yorkshire, where she spends most of her time.

In Holland, Robbert J.B. Koopman, Toto's nephew, provided many details about his family, as well as several photographs from his personal albums. His help was very meaningful, to say the least.

And, as ever, I wish to express my deep affection and gratitude to my friend Liane Viguié-Cohen.

Notes

1. Delay, Claude. *Giacometti, Alberto et Diego. L'histoire cachée.* Paris: Fayard, 2007. 271.

2. Charles Roux, Edmonde. *Chanel and Her World.* New York: Vendome Press, 2005. 272.

3. *Ibid,* 273.

4. Keenan, Brigid. *The Women We Wanted to Look Like.* New York: St. Martin's Press, 1978. 11.

5. Ewing, William A. *The Photographic Art of Hoyningen-Huene.* New York: Rizzoli, 1986. 101.

6. Trefusis, Violet. *Prelude to Misadventure.* London: Hutchinson, 1941. 14.

7. Chisholm, Anne and Michael Davie. *Lord Beaverbrook: A Life.* New York: Alfred A. Knopf, 1993. 317.

8. *Ibid,* 318.

9. After the war, Toto Koopman was advised to file a report in order to receive compensation for her suffering. She gathered evidence to support her case, and that is how William Rospigliosi, a correspondent for Time-Life International Group in Rome, came to write the report that was filed by the law offices of Elvy Robb and Co. in London.

10. Richardson, John. *The Sorcerer's Apprentice: Picasso, Provence and Douglas Cooper*. New York: Alfred A. Knopf, 1999. 77. He places the action in a camp outside of Padua, while in fact it was in the Perugia area.

11. Amicale de Ravensbrück et Association des Deportées et Internées de la Résistance. *Les Françaises à Ravensbrück*. Paris: Gallimard, 1965. 110.

12. *Ibid*, 117.

13. Original text from Toto's letter.

14. Amicale de Ravensbrück et Association des Deportées et Internées de la Résistance. *op. cit.*, 173.

15. Tillion, Germaine. *La Traversée du mal*. Paris: Arléa, 2000. 81-82.

16. *The Independent* (September 4, 1991) and *The Daily Telegraph* (September 18, 1991).

17. Peppiatt, Michael *Francis Bacon: Anatomy of an Enigma*. New York: Farrar, Straus and Giroux, 1997. 115.

18. *Ibid*, 131.

19. *Ibid*, 144.

20. An allusion to *Ubu Roi (Ubu the King)*, a play by Alfred Jarry. Ubu is a portly, unattractive and boorish character.

21. Barbara was a French singer and songwriter (1930-1997).

Selected Bibliography

Amicale de Ravensbrück et Association des Déportées et Internées de la Résistance, *Les Françaises à Ravensbrück*. Paris: Gallimard, 1965.

Anderson, Margaret. *The Unknowable Gurdjieff*. London: Routledge, 1962.

Berberova, Nina. *Histoire de la baronne Boudberg*. Arles: Actes Sud, 1998.

Bergonzi, Bernard. *Reading the Thirties*. London: Macmillan, 1978.

Berthoud, Roger. *Graham Sutherland*. London: Faber & Faber, 1982.

Beyeler, Ernst. *Fondation Beyeler*. London and New York: Prestel, 1997.

Bret, David. *Tallulah Bankhead: A Scandalous Life*. London: Robson Books, 1996.

Brook, Peter. *Threads of Time*. Washington: Counterpoint, 1998.

Burke, Carolyn. *Lee Miller: A Life*. New York: Alfred A. Knopf, 2005.

Cave Brown, Anthony. *The Secret Servant: The Life of Sir Stewart Menzies, Churchill's Spymaster*. London: Michael Joseph, 1988.

Charles-Roux, Edmonde. *Chanel and Her World*. New York: Vendome Press, 2005.

Chisholm, Anne and Michael Davie. *Lord Beaverbrook: A Life*. New York: Alfred A. Knopf, 1993.

Crosby, Caresse. *The Passionate Years*. New York: The Dial Press, 1953.

Delay, Claude. *Giacometti, Alberto et Diego. L'histoire cachée*. Paris: Fayard, 2007.

Ewing, William A. *The Photographic Art of Hoyningen-Huene*. New York: Rizzoli, 1986.

Farson, Daniel. *Francis Bacon. Aspects d'une vie*. Paris: Le Promeneur, 1994.

Gaulle-Anthonioz, Geneviève de. *La traversée de la nuit*. Paris: Le Seuil, 1998.

Ghirshman, Tania. *Archéologue malgré moi*. Paris: Albin Michel, 1970.

Gimpel, René. *Diary of an Art Dealer*. London: Hamish Hamilton, 1986.

Keenan, Brigid. *The Women We Wanted to Look Like*. New York: St. Martin's Press, 1978.

Leslie, Anita. *Cousin Randolph: The Life of Randolph Churchill*. London: Hutchinson, 1985.

McCall, Henrietta. *The Life of Max Mallowan: Archaeology and Agatha Christie*. London: British Museum Press, 2001.

Mallowan, Max. *Mallowan's Memoirs*. London: Collins, 1977.

Mann, Carol. *Paris Between the Wars*. New York: Vendome Press, 1996.

Mason, Raymond. *Art et artistes*. Turin: Edizioni d'Arte Fratelli Pozzo, 2000.

Moore, James. *Gurdjieff: The Anatomy of a Myth*. Shaftesbury: Element, 1991.

Pauwels, Louis. *Monsieur Gurdjieff*. Paris: Albin Michel, 1996.

Penrose, Antony. *The Lives of Lee Miller*. London: Thames and Hudson, 1995.

Peppiatt, Michael. *Francis Bacon: Anatomy of an Enigma*. New York: Farrar, Straus and Giroux, 1997.

Queneau, Raymond. *Journaux 1914-1965*. Paris: Gallimard, 1996.

Richardson, John. *The Sorcerer's Apprentice: Picasso, Provence and Douglas Cooper*. New York: Alfred A. Knopf, 1999.

Rothenstein, John. *Time's Thievish Progress*. London: Cassell, 1970.

Saint-Pern, Dominique de. *Les amants du soleil noir, Harry et Caresse Crosby*. Paris: Grasset, 2005.

Saint-Phalle, Niki de. *Traces, une autobiographie*. Paris: Acatos, 1999.

Shakespeare, Nicholas. *Bruce Chatwin*. London: Harvill Press, 1999.

Sitwell, Edith. *Selected Letters*, edited by Richard Greene. London: Virago Press, 1997.

Sorensen, Colin. *London on Film*. London: Museum of London, 1996.

Tillion, Germaine. *La traversée du mal*. Paris: Arléa, 2000.

Trefusis, Violet. *Prelude to Misadventure*. London: Hutchinson, 1941.

Tual, Denise. *Au coeur du temps*. Paris: Carrère, 1990.

Webb, James. *The Harmonious Circle: The Lives and Work of G. I. Gurdjieff, P. D. Ouspensky and Their Followers*. New York: Putnam, 1980.

Webb, Peter. *Portrait of David Hockney*. London: Chatto & Windus, 1988.

Wellington-Koo, Hui-Lan. *No Feast Lasts Forever*. New York: New York Times Books, 1975.

Werbell, Frederick E. and Clarke Thurston. *Wallenberg, le héros disparu*. Paris: Belfond, 1987.